AN INTRODUCTION TO THE STUDY OF THE RELATIONS OF INDIAN STATES WITH THE GOVERNMENT OF INDIA

AN INTRODUCTION TO THE STUDY OF THE RELATIONS OF INDIAN STATES WITH THE GOVERNMENT OF INDIA

BY

K.M. PANIKKAR, B.A. (Oxon.)

GYAN

Published by

Gyan Publishing House
5, Ansari Road
Daryaganj, New Delhi-110002
Phone: 011-47034999, 9811692060
E-mail: books@gyanbooks.com

Distribution Network
gyanbooks.com
India, USA, Canada, UK, Australia

ISBN: 978-81-212-7617-7 (PB)
First Published, 1927

2nd Impression 2024

Printed at: Gyan Press, Delhi.

AN INTRODUCTION TO THE STUDY OF THE RELATIONS OF INDIAN STATES WITH THE GOVERNMENT OF INDIA

Author: K.M. PANIKKAR

AN INTRODUCTION TO THE STUDY OF THE RELATIONS OF INDIAN STATES WITH THE GOVERNMENT OF INDIA

AN INTRODUCTION TO THE STUDY OF THE RELATIONS OF INDIAN STATES WITH THE GOVERNMENT OF INDIA

BY

K. M. PANIKKAR, B.A. (Oxon.)

DIXON SCHOLAR OF CHRIST CHURCH, OXFORD
SOME TIME SENIOR PROFESSOR OF HISTORY, MUSLIM UNIVERSITY, ALIGARH
FELLOW OF THE INDIAN WOMEN'S UNIVERSITY AND LATE EDITOR
'HINDUSTAN TIMES,' DELHI

LONDON: MARTIN HOPKINSON
& COMPANY LTD: 14 HENRIETTA
STREET, COVENT GARDEN, W.C. 1927

CONTENTS

INTRODUCTION

THE purpose of this book is not political in the ordinary sense of the word. It is not an attempt either to justify the existence of Indian states or to attack their methods of government. My object has been to analyse and interpret the unique system of polity that has developed in India, partly as a result of policy and partly as a result of historical accident. The internal states of India and their relation with the British Government afford no parallel or analogy to any institution known to history. The political system they represent is neither feudal nor federal, though in some aspects it shows similarities to both which have misguided alike the statesman and the political thinker. It is not an international system, though the principal states in India are bound to the British Government by solemn treaties and are spoken of in official documents as allies. Nor would it be correct to consider it a political confederacy in which the major partner has assumed special rights, because it is admitted by all parties that the constituent states have no rights of secession.

A polity so curious and so unique deserves to be studied and analysed without any other direct political motive than that of scientific interest. Unfortunately, from thinkers and writers on political law it has not so far received the attention it deserves. Sir William Lee Warner, who is the only writer of any consequence who attempted to deal with this problem, was an eminent member of the Indian Civil Service, and he was naturally much impressed by the Roman analogy and pushed it to the length of claiming for the paramount power unlimited right of authority over the states. A purely objective attitude was impossible in his case, and his book, extremely valuable though it be for the inside information which it contains, is hardly more than a justification of the claims of the political department. Sir Charles Tupper's book on the Indian Protectorate is an avowed attempt to establish the feudal theory, which even the Government of India have never officially sought to put forward. He sees in the relation between the paramount power and the states all the important elements of feudalism. Says he, 'If the fiefs were isolated, so are the native states. If the holders of the fiefs enjoyed immunity from the laws of any external power, so in general do the chiefs exercising various degrees of internal sovereignty. Even in the methods by which the system of protectorate had been gradually formed we see likeness to the process of feudalisation.'[1] Whatever other interpretation, the relationship between the British Government and the Indian states may bear, it certainly is not feudal, nor

[1] Tupper, *Our Indian Protectorate*, London, 1893, p. 239.

could the historical circumstances by which the Nizams of Hyderabad, the Rajahs of Travancore, the Rulers of Bhopal and the Scindias of Gwalior came to be allied for purposes of defence, be described as processes of feudalisation. The word feudatory, which was loosely used in earlier times, was probably responsible for so untenable a theory, which, however, finds no advocates in any quarter now.

No other work of any importance besides these two has been attempted. The need for a new study has long been felt. The position of the princes has considerably changed during the last seven years, and the feeling has gained ground that the system of public law, which governs the relations between the Government and the states, is a complicated labyrinth to which it would be unwise and impolitic to apply any uniform principle. The tendency of an earlier generation was towards uniformity, to apply to all alike a code of political practice developed from precedent and theory. This has now been given up, and it has been publicly recognised that the relations of each state with the paramount power will be decided purely by reference to individual agreements and treaties or on the basis of general principles accepted by the Princes' Chamber. The theory that the rights and privileges of states are derived directly or indirectly from the paramount power, and are not inherent—a position which Lord Curzon took up in his public speeches—has also been given up. It is now recognised that the obligations are bilateral, at least in the case of treaty states, in contrast with states created by grant or Sanad. A new position has hence arisen which is more in accordance with historical facts, which makes a re-statement of the position necessary. My endeavour in this study has been merely to present the facts and analyse as best I could the political system that is based on them.

To the student of political science the subject is one of special interest. It raises so many questions with regard to the nature of sovereignty, the basis of law, the position of the judiciary in subordinate states, that an examination of the subject in all its aspects would illuminate almost every side of political theory. Nowhere has the division of sovereign attributes been carried to such an extent. The Indian states include among them every variety of political community ranging from a full-powered sovereign state, like Hyderabad or Gwalior, whose rulers enjoy legally 'unrestrained powers'[1] of life and death over their subjects, and who make, promulgate and enforce their own laws and maintain their own armies, to small chieftainships of a few square miles of territory. Though the rulers of the bigger states are subordinate[2] to the Government of India, their laws are supreme in their own state, and there is no appeal from their courts even to the Privy Council. The writ of His Majesty does

[1] *Lord Chelmsford's Speeches*, vol. ii. pp. 150-1.
[2] *Ibid.*

not run in the states, and the surrender of criminals is governed by separate agreements. The states of India have been a standing repudiation of the Austinian principle of sovereignty, and it is after his direct experience of them that Sir Henry Maine came so strenuously to hold that sovereignty is divisible, and to deny emphatically the conception that has persisted through centuries in European political thought, that sovereignty is one, indivisible and inalienable. I must admit beforehand that no attempt is made in this book to discuss these theoretical questions beyond presenting a few facts which may have an interesting bearing on them.

Two things make the study difficult. First, there is the vagueness of the term Indian states, which brings under one category a full-powered treaty state, like Hyderabad or Gwalior, and a chief holding a fief under a grant from the paramount power and the lord of a petty estate in Kathiawad. The attempt to classify all the states under one heading has been the cause of much confusion. It is impossible to find anything like common ground between the chief of Ilchalkaranji or the Nawab of Banganapalle and the Nizam of Hyderabad or the Gaekwar of Baroda. Yet in the popular mind, and till recently to a large extent in the practice of the political department, these rulers were really members of the same class and stood in very nearly the same relation to the Government of India. They were all alike classed as feudatories and their territories as 'Native States.' A classification more closely approximating to facts is the first necessity in the study of the relations between the Government of India and the states. But this is not so easy as it looks. A century of political practice has altered the original character of many states, and a classification based on rights is possible only on a close examination of the secret archives of the political department of the Government of India. In fact, when the full-powered princes made an attempt to establish such a differentiation as a preliminary to the constitution of the Princes' Chamber, Lord Chelmsford pointed out that the course suggested would be impossible, and that the salute list, imperfect as it was, was the only available method of classification. However that be, the first thing necessary to keep in mind in the study of problems relating to Indian states is that the relationship of no one state with the Government is like that of another, though a broad differentiation based on similarity of historical circumstances may be traced by which it would be found that the princes and chiefs fall into three distinct classifications—those whose treaties entitle them to full and absolute sovereignty within the state, those who, though treaty states, enjoy criminal and civil jurisdiction and legislative powers only under supervision, and those whose rights are based on grants and sanads. This broad line of distinction is the main fact that has to be kept in mind in studying the question of Indian states.

The second and more difficult thing that stands

in the way of a proper study of this question is the absence of any regular sources of information. The Government of India has always treated the subject as a sacred mystery. The practices and precedents with regard to each state differ greatly, and even Indian Dewans with direct experience of political dealings naturally come to know only how the particular state with which they are connected stands in relation to the Government of India. There is, of course, no secrecy about the actual treaty or the main agreements that supplement it. But notoriously the political law of India is not governed solely by treaties or by agreements, but by a complex code which is the accumulation of practice in the political department. Indeed, the political usages and customs which govern the relations of the states with the Government form a kind of semi-international law which is too delicate to codify and too complex to be analysed. Strictly speaking, they do not form a constitutional law in the Austinian sense of being 'a compound of positive morality and positive law which fixes the structure of a government.' Neither can they be described as being a part of international law. No Indian state can quote the principles of international law or precedents in its relations with the British Government. Though, for purposes of persuasion and elucidation, it is often done, however conclusive in its application, it is not considered binding on either party. Tupper, indeed, holds that the practice of the political department is positive law, as it can be enforced by the paramount power. No Indian state with full internal autonomy would accept this view or even concede the *right* of the Government to enforce its political practice, though on the basis of superior force the states have often to yield to the dictates of Simla. The Nizam in his letter to the Viceroy dated the 25th of October, 1923, put forward this point of view in the following terms: The rejection by H.M.'s Government of his claim to the restoration of the Berars 'can only be a fact expressing its view, but it cannot impose upon me or on my house the obligation to treat the subject as closed or regard the claim as barred for all time.'[1] But that does not establish a legal sanction, and the major part of the principles by which the relations of the states and the Government are governed are no more positive law than are the customs and agreements which exist between independent political communities. With regard to certain fundamental and basic conceptions this would not, however, be wholly true. There are certain constitutional facts which are acknowledged alike by the princes and by the Government which no ruler can question or deny, such as the prohibition of private war, the limitation of armaments, etc., a breach of which would give the paramount power the *right* to enforce legal sanctions. This point was emphasised by the Viceroy in the recent correspondence between the Government of India and

[1] East India Correspondence—Hyberabad, Continuation of Cmd., 2439, p. 4.

the Nizam. The Nizam had claimed that in regard to internal matters his government was independent and on a position of equality with the British Government. He denied the right of the British to make binding decisions on matters relating to his controversies with the Government of India. Lord Reading's reply, which was textually approved by the Secretary of State, declared, 'I regret I cannot accept your Exalted Highness's view that the orders of the Secretary of State on your representation do not amount to a decision. It is the right and privilege of the paramount power to decide all disputes that may arise between states or between one of the states and itself.'[1] But this principle has to some extent been recognised even in international law, especially in the covenant of the League of Nations, which lays down the principle of international action in case of a breach of obligation. On these specific matters something like a positive public law is traceable; but the great majority of questions that arise in the daily relation of Indian states with the Government have nothing to do with these basic principles. On those matters usage and custom are extraordinarily varied and complex, and in many cases merely inchoate. This is what makes a comprehensive and authoritative study, except by one who has occupied responsible positions in the political department, absolutely impossible.

At this present time no elaborate plea for the existence of Indian states or even a justification of

[1] *Ibid.*

their existence is necessary. They are political facts which, whether we like them or not, stare us in the face and to a large extent govern the course of our political evolution. While their faults are many and the difficulties that their position raises grave, there can be no doubt that they add greatly to the richness and variety of India's national life and fill a position which has politically and culturally a value of its own. From the point of view of the British Government their importance has long been recognised. Sir John Malcolm, one of the most talented of Anglo-Indian statesmen, whose knowledge of Indian states was unique in many respects, declared so long ago as 1825, 'I am decidedly of opinion that the tranquillity not to say the security of our vast oriental possessions is involved in the preservation of native principalities which are dependent on us for protection. These are also so obviously at our mercy, so entirely within our grasp that besides other and great benefits we derive from their alliances their co-existence with our rule is of itself a source of political strength, the value of which will never be known till it is lost.' The political value from the standpoint of the Government has been well recognised since the Mutiny. The active services, political and military, of the princes during the Great War have emphasised the wisdom of that policy, and the Government have lost no opportunity to make it clear that they realise in full the value of maintaining the princes in their dignity and guaranteeing them in full measure their rights and their powers. But in the mind of the Indian people as a whole there has been a suspicion, altogether unjust, that the states are maintained by the Government as instruments against the just rights of the country. Being, as Sir John Malcolm said, so utterly at the mercy of the Government and dependent entirely on the guarantee of the paramount power for their continued enjoyment of authority and rights, the interests of the rulers of Indian states have been so far to support the Government in any action it took. But from the Indian point of view the justification of the existence of Indian states lies not in the attitude the princes take up on questions of immediate political interest, but in two other directions. First of all, until recently the internal states provided opportunities for Indians to demonstrate and develop their capacity for political and administrative matters. They provided a school for Indian statesmanship. While Indians were practically confined to subordinate appointments in British India, and the argument was frequently heard that they lacked both capacity and character for higher work, the Indian states alone offered fields for men of capacity. The career and achievements of statesmen and administrators like Sir T. Madhava Rao, Sir Salar Jung, Sir Dinkar Rao, Sir Seshadri Aiyar, and Sankunni Menon, amply justify, if nothing else does, the existence of these states. That even now the states afford opportunities denied in British India is clear at least on one point—a military career in the fullest degree for

Indians. Most of the larger Indian states maintain armies which are officered entirely by Indians who receive their training under European military advisers. In Mysore, Hyderabad, Baroda, Gwalior, Indore, Bikanir, Patiala, Kashmir and other states, there are local military establishments of a high grade of efficiency, which are commanded and controlled by Indians. The military spirit that has almost died out among the peoples of British India is being kept alive in these states where men of birth and family may still enter the profession of arms and earn distinction as Maharajah Sir Pertab Singh and the late Maharajah of Gwalior did in the defence of their motherland. Even in the purely political career the states even now afford opportunities of initiative and talent seldom available in British India, and not a few of the men who have made their mark in British India, as Sir P. Rajagopala Chari and Sir M. Visweswarayya, have had their training in the affairs of Indian states. The opportunity for talents which the states afford, which has produced even in the present day men like Sir A. R. Bannerjea, Sir Manubhai Mehta, Nawab Hyder Nawaz Jung and Colonel Haksar, and among the rulers themselves men of the capacity of the late Maharajahs of Gwalior and Travancore and the reigning Maharajahs of Mysore, Baroda and Bikaner, cannot be brushed aside as unimportant. The demand for self-government has had no greater argument in its support than the general success of the rule of the princes in their own states and the happiness of the people living under their care, though there have been notorious cases of misrule, tyranny and oppression which have marred the effect and obscured the impression of the high level of success attained in many states.

Besides this, the states and their rulers have been custodians of our cultural and artistic tradition in a degree that we cannot appreciate now. The very conservatism of the rulers has been of value in this connection. In the midst of a changing and disintegrating society, their states have in many cases preserved the solidarity of the social structure and kept intact the imperceptible bonds that unite classes and castes into one community. That is the explanation of the almost total absence of communal antagonism except that which is directly encouraged or imported from British India. The Maharajahs of Kashmir have been orthodox Hindus ruling over a Muslim population. The population in the Nizam's dominions is predominantly Hindu; and though of recent times there have been occasional riots, the relations between the communities have been on the whole extraordinarily good. Village life is vigorous, and there is almost undisturbed social harmony. This obviously is not due either to efficient administration—for in many states such a thing is unknown—or as a result of a purposive policy, for the rulers in many cases unfortunately have only their pleasures and their sport at heart. A more fundamental cause has to be sought, and that, in my opinion, is found in the fact that society has continued practically undisturbed in these areas, while in British India new currents of life and new and changing political and social conditions have tended to disorganise and render ineffective the unseen forces behind the structure of the community. This is certainly not all to our advantage, for progress can come only through purposive evolution, and a static society must tend to weigh down both individuality and activity through the leaden weight of encrusted custom. But all the same, a conservative tradition has much in its favour, especially in the midst of a society which is changing fast through the contact of dissimilar cultures. Moreover, to a large extent the states have served the cause of India's civilisation by acting as a refuge of certain valuable forms of intellectual activity which, through one circumstance or another, could not find adequate support in British India. Especially in the development of vernaculars, through which alone can education ever reach the mass mind of India, the states and their governments have rendered a common service. The Nizam's government has founded a university in which the course of instruction is entirely in Urdu. The encouragement given by the Mysore university to Canarese and by Travancore to Malayalam has gone a great way in modernising those languages. Indian music and architecture survive now mostly in the states and find their patrons mainly among the more old-fashioned rulers and noblemen. It is true that in a few cases like Kapurthala and Kooch Bihar the

Maharajahs may seem to have taken to ultra-modern things, but they are exceptions which help more to emphasise the conservatism of the other rulers than to obscure it.

If there are undoubted advantages of this kind there are also considerable disadvantages. The seamy side of the ordinary prince's life needs no emphasis here. An occasional incident causes to be thrown on the court life of Indian princes a glare of light which exposes it to the gaze of all the world. It is not part of our purpose here to go into it. The only thing we have to note in connection with the degraded luxury and the meaningless pomp of many Indian courts is that such a result is inevitable when there is no sense of direct responsibility in the princes. In olden times a despot who oppressed his subjects or a debauchee who looked only to his pleasure was not left long undisturbed. Either an outside invasion or an internal rebellion put an end to his career. But the British Government now supports the ruler as long as he is loyal to his agreement and does not too openly violate civilised conventions. The ruler is left free in such a case to do whatever he pleases with his treasury and to fleece his subjects to any extent for the sake of his pleasures. What is really objectionable and leads to much of the misgovernment of the states is the failure on the part of a great many of the rulers to distinguish between their private income and the revenues of the state. A good many of them look upon their dominions with a proprietor's feeling. To my knowledge one important ruler used always to allude to his territories as 'my Estate.' It is this feeling of proprietary authority in the case of a large number of princes that leads them to an inadequate appreciation of the financial needs of government and a largely exaggerated view of their own necessities.

More important than this, and entirely unconnected with the personality of the rulers, is the question of the rights of the state subjects. The state subjects, we are told, have a dual allegiance; one to their immediate ruler and the other indirectly to the paramount power. But they seem to have no rights as against either. If an autocratic ruler confiscates property and arrests and imprisons for no reason, there is no court to which appeal can be made and no authority which will uphold just rights. I do not suggest that all Indian rulers do this. There are many states like Mysore and Travancore in which constitutional government has been established over a long period and where the subjects enjoy perfect freedom of person and property and security from aggression. But it is notorious that there are many states in which as against the ruler the subjects have no right whatever. The most elementary rights may be denied to them. In ordinary cases the British Government would hear no petition, nor in any but the most exceptional could it take any effective action. While under the rule of the princes the ryots as a whole are undeniably happy—political rights and liberties have but little to do with the happiness of the ordinary citizen—it cannot be denied that the political position of the subjects of these states is anomalous and altogether lacks the ordinary guarantees of a free man's life. This is really at the root of educated India's hostility towards the princes. Unless the princes as a whole realise that they have duties as well as prerogatives, that their subjects are entitled to the largest amount of freedom and the most unhampered exercise of civil rights compatible with the safety of the community, that persons and rights are inviolable, progressive thought in India will look upon them with suspicion. The crux of the problem of the princes so far as Indians are concerned lies here.

That, however, is outside the scope of my work. My purpose is merely to study the relations subsisting between the princes and the Government of India, and their future evolution. I have rigidly kept out all matter, however interesting, which has no bearing on the problem before me. I can only hope that the book would be found interesting both by professional students of politics and by the lay reader. Indian politicians have so far sadly neglected this problem, and if my work helps in the least to focus the attention of the political world of India upon this all-important question, I shall feel recompensed.

I

EARLY DAYS

THE problem of Indian states, though in its present form it is almost entirely a result of the British occupation and is connected with the history and accidents of British growth, has in some respects existed all through Indian history. The imperial dynasties of ancient times in India had to deal with their *samantas* and local chiefs in the same way, and we have evidence in Asoka's inscriptions of the differentiation between border states under 'political influence' and internal states with limited autonomous rights. The same may be said of the time of the Guptas, whose imperial sway extended over India for more than two and a half centuries. The detailed descriptions of Yuan Chwang leave us no doubt that Harsha's political system was also based on a consolidation of local rulers by alliance and conquest, and some of them, like the Kumara Raja of Kamarupa, were left semi-independent with obligations to the *parameswara* or the emperor. In fact, the Hindu ideal of *samrajya* was not that of a state which directly administered all the territory over which it laid claim to sovereignty but of a powerful homeland under direct control with rights of sovereignty and tribute over local rulers or *samantas*. This system was inherited by the Mussulmans who from policy continued it, as an effective reduction of all Hindu princes would have demanded a stability and military organisation beyond the resources of the Pathan adventurers who set themselves up as the Sultans of Delhi. The question of the relations of these states to the central power was seriously considered only by the Moghuls who, under the great Akbar, enunciated a definite policy in relation to them. He left the rulers of Rajputana and of Bundlekund undisturbed, provided they accepted the sovereignty and authority of the emperor, and derived their rights from the Moghul throne. Though the Rajput rajas were *de facto* ruling princes, their claim to be independent rulers was never admitted by the Moghuls who exercised the right of wardship, succession and deposition. Successive Moghul emperors from Akbar exacted obeisance from their Hindu rajas who enjoyed ruling rights, punished disloyalty, rewarded the faithful and gave titles of distinction. Their claim to royalty was not recognised, and in relation to the Padshas they were only subjects like the rest.

But with the decline of the Moghul power these local rulers asserted and maintained their independence, and when the East India Company began to deal with them directly, they found them *de facto* sovereigns of their states though rendering a nominal allegiance to the throne of Delhi. The chief Indian powers with whom the Company came into contact were the viceroys and governors of the Moghuls whose subordinate relation with the descendant of Akbar and Aurangazib could not be disputed either in fact or in theory. But the position of the Company as an Indian power was the same. The Grant of the Diwani converted the Company into a Governorship in Commission, and naturally the treaties with the Wazir of Oudh, the Nizam of Hyderabad and others were as between equals. The same causes that helped the Company to attain the Empire in India worked for the acquisition of independence by these princes. More than that, in the early stages of its fight for dominion, especially with the French and with the Mysore Sultan, the Company was to a large extent dependent upon the co-operation and support of Indian states like the Nizam and the Nawab of Arcot who were in alliance with it. Thus there came about the rights of independence and sovereignty which have given the immemorial problem of local rulers in India a new political and legal aspect.

That at the end of the eighteenth century and the beginning of the nineteenth, the chief Indian states, like the Mahrattas and the Nizam, were even in the strictest Austinian sense, independent sovereigns, could not be questioned. It is true that no one except Tipu took the title of king, but that was due to the same policy which led the East India Company claim merely to be ruling on the basis of the Emperor's firman. In India it was the age of camouflaged royalty, when independent sovereigns with rights of peace and war and absolute and unrestrained dominion claimed to be merely slipper-bearers and servants. The best example of this system was the fact that till the very last, the Peishwa who had reduced the descendant of Sivaji to the position of a pensioner, was content with the title of Pandit Pradhan, and his succession had to be regularly recognised by his nominal sovereign at Satara. When a Brahmin envoy of Haider Ali to the court of Poona was reproached for representing an usurper, it was mildly pointed out that he was only following the example of more illustrious durbars. When Mahadaji Scindia, who was the virtual ruler of Northern India, visited Poona, he took with him a pair of slippers which he humbly placed before the Peishwa and stood with naked feet at a distance. One further instance will show how far this fiction was carried. In 1803 when Sicunder Jah ascended the *gadi* in Hyderabad, he had it recognised by the King of Delhi, who was virtually a prisoner and in fact a pensioner of the British with whom the Nizam was in equal alliance.

Thus the problem of Indian states is partly inherited and partly the creation of the same set of circumstances which helped to establish British power in India. The rapid changes in the fortunes of the Company, which in the short space of fifty years obtained complete dominion over India, led to a system of complicated relationship with the states, which can only be explained in the light of its historical growth. The different phases of treaty relations were due mostly to the different conditions of the Company's fortunes, and thus by a rapid process the treaty of mutual friendship and reciprocal obligations entered into with the earlier allies, such as the Nizam and the Rajah of Travancore, slowly become treaties of subordinate co-operation and one-sided obligation as in the Treaty of Udaipur in 1819, and the grant by the grace of the sovereign power as in the case of Indore in 1844, when the succession by adoption to the Holkar's *gadi* was sanctioned on the condition that he should derive his authority 'from being placed there by the British Government.'[1]

The historical growth of the system of native states in treaty relationship to the East India Company and by succession to the crown may now be traced. The East India Company acquired the right of belligerency with non-Christian powers by the Charter of Charles II. This gave them the legal authority to negotiate engagements, alliances and treaties. Such agreements were not subject to the jurisdiction of courts. This was decided in 1793 when Lord Commissioner Eyre, in his Chancery judgment in the action brought by Nawab Mahommed Ali of Arcot, decided that the treaties between the Company and the states were not a subject of private municipal jurisdiction. The first treaty entered into by the East India Company with an

[1] Despatch from the Government of India to the Court of Directors, dated 23rd December, 1844, para. 10.

This was abrogated later on.

Indian state was the Treaty of Anjengo with the Rajah of Travancore, which was negotiated by Dr. Alexander Orme, the historian's father, who was the chief of the Anjengo factory. The treaty, which was signed in 1723, was for the purpose of erecting a fort in Collache, for which the Company was to supply the artillery and munitions. The treaty also declared that the Government of the Rajah will be in league and united in *good friendship with* the Honourable East India Company.[1] The next treaty of importance was with Savantwadi on 12th January, 1730, which was a defensive and offensive agreement against Angria, the notorious pirate, who infested the west coast at that time. The same object of putting down piracy led the Company into an alliance with Jinjira in 1733. These three treaties, it will be noticed, are with minor chieftains for a purely local purpose and have no political significance beyond the maintenance of conditions conducive to the Company's local trade. The first agreement of a general character with an important Indian power was the maritime and commercial treaty negotiated with the Poona Court, by which the Company was conceded free trade in the dominions ruled by the Peishwa. This was in the nature of a political gain as it was the result of the successful resistance against Kanoji Angria and his sons, and of the consequent development of British sea power in Bombay. But this treaty, though it

[1] Quoted in *History of Kerala* by K. P. Padmanabha Menon, Cochin Government Press, 1924, p. 338.

was a sign of the increasing political prestige of the Company, was only a commercial agreement. The logic of events was fast compelling the Company to stand forth as one of the political powers in the peninsula. The war of Austrian succession soon became, so far as England and France were concerned, a race for Colonial power, and the genius of Dupleix forced the issue in the Coromandal Coast. The conflict that followed did not end even with the Peace of Aix la Chapelle, but continued till the British Company emerged triumphant with their nominee, Nawab Mahommed Ali, ruling as the Subedar of Arcot.

The first political treaty which demonstrated the changed character of the Company following this victory and the victory of Plassey was the agreement of mutual neutrality negotiated with the Subedar of Hyderabad on the 14th of May, 1759. In South India the rivalry between Haider Ali, the Nizam and the Mahrattas had created a balance of power; and this gave the Company an importance which was reflected in the Treaty of Masulipatam, by which the Company entered into a military alliance with the Nizam. This may be said to be the beginning of the policy of definite alliance with Indian states for the maintenance of political power. In the north the treaty with the Nawab of Murshidabad left him a puppet.

From this time up to the time of the Marquis of Wellesley the East India Company is only one of the powers in India, and the treaties and alliances it entered into were for the purpose of maintaining its position against its rivals. The other states which were powerful enough to contest the authority of the Company were the Mahrattas who, though weakened by the defeat of Panipat, were still the most considerable people in India, Mysore, which under Haider Ali had become a powerful empire, and the Suba of the Deccan, which under Asaf Jah's successors was consolidating Mussulman power in the Deccan. All through there was also the French menace, which was never completely eliminated till the defeat of Perron's forces in 1803. The first British alliance of a subsidiary character was with princes in immediate contiguity to the Company's territories, and was frankly for the purpose of defence against the attack of these three Indian powers. The subsidiary alliances developed as a defensive system by which the Company, anxious for its trade, determined on the defence, not of its own boundaries, but of the state next to it in geographical position. This policy was later on described by Lord Salisbury as that of defending the moon in order to ward off an attack on the Earth from Mars. It is necessary to keep this principle clearly in mind in studying the history of alliances with the Carnatic, Oudh and the Nizam.

The first of these subsidiary treaties was made with the Nawab Wazir of Oudh. The treaty was made after the British troops had made a triumphal entry into Lucknow. If the policy and military strength of the Company permitted, it could have then annexed the dominions over which Shuja ud Dowla ruled. But the circumstances in which the Company were placed did not permit of such a course. It would have given the British merchants an extensive land frontier, which they would have had to defend against the Duranees from Afghanistan and the Mahrattas from the Deccan. The Company was at that time powerless to undertake a military responsibility of this kind, owing to its financial weakness. The result was the subsidiary alliance by which Shuja ud Dowla was restored to authority in Oudh. The defence of the Oudh frontier was recognised to be a matter of vital concern to the Company, and the second clause of the treaty laid it down thus: 'In case the Dominions of H.H. Shuja ud Dowla at any time hereafter be attacked . . . the East India Company shall assist him with a part or whole of their forces. In the case of the English Company's forces being employed in His Highness's service the extraordinary expenses of the same to be defrayed by him.'[1]

This clause clearly explains the purpose and the policy of the Company. The East India Company realised that the defence of the frontier of Oudh was the only safe defence for them, and took the responsibility for holding it against hostile attack; but the expenses of this was to be borne by the Nawab. The subsidiary system began thus as a method of defence without expenditure. 'The defence of the Nawab's possession from

[1] Aitchison, *Treaties and Sanads* (4th ed.), 1909.

invasion is in fact the defence of ours,' said Warren Hastings.[1]

The Duke of Wellington (then merely Sir Arthur Wellesley), writing forty years later on the question of the importance of Oudh to the Company's defences, pointed out that by ' this intimate union, a barrier was provided for the Provinces under the Bengal Government. Nothing remained on the left or east of the Ganges besides the Nawab of Oudh and the Company excepting the Rohillas, and this river afforded a strong natural barrier against all invaders. Besides this object, the seat of war in consequence with the alliance with the possession of Oudh was removed from the Company's provinces . . . to those of the Nawab if such supposed war should have been reduced to the defensive.'

The Nawab Wazir was guaranteed absolute internal independence, which in fact he possessed at that time. But as the strength of the Company increased and his military power declined, he soon sank to the position of a vassal ruler. By the time of Hastings the Wazir had come ' to subsist on British strength entirely,'[2] and this gave the Company the opportunity to make further demands on him and to alter the treaties to their advantage. By the Treaty of Benares, which Hastings concluded with Shuja ud Dowla, Oudh was converted practically into a province of the Company for whose internal government it refused to be responsible. Both the Marquis

[1] Letter to Col. Champion, Gleig, i. 443.

[2] Letter to Lawrence Sullivan, Gleig, i. 356.

of Cornwallis and Sir John Shore continued this policy so effectively that Sir Arthur Wellesley remarked caustically, that the stipulation of internal independence had been uniformly frustrated by the necessarily uniform interference of the Company in all those concerns for the support of the Nawab's authority, for the preservation of tranquillity in the country and for the security of the funds from which the Company derived so important a portion of the resources applicable to the payment of their military establishment.[1]

Thus, when the Marquis of Wellesley came out as Governor-General, the Wazir's military position was a serious embarrassment to him, and as a result, after considerable pressure, a new treaty was signed, the purpose of which, as thc Marquis himself (then Earl of Mornington) declared in his despatch,[2] dated 28th November, 1799, to the Court of Directors, was to 'establish the sole and exclusive authority of the Company within the Province of Oudh and its dependencies.' The new treaty negotiated by Henry Wellesley and Colonel Scott isolated the territorial possessions of the Wazir, by annexing to the direct government of the Company the Doab and reserved for the Governor-General 'the positive right of interference in the internal management of the Country retained by the Nawab.'[3] The first native

[1] *Wellesley Despatches*, edited by S. J. Owen, Oxford, MDCCCLXXVII, page lxxxiii.

[2] *Wellesley Despatches*, 188.

[3] *Wellesley Despatches*, Letter to the Secret Committee of the Court of Directors, dated 14th November, 1801.

state was thus established, and a new system came into being.

The history of the Carnatic was similar. The Nawabs of Arcot were established on the Musnad solely by British support. But as in the case of Oudh in the early days there was no attempt to restrict the internal authority or the external relations of the Nawab. In fact, a regular ambassador (Sir T. Rumbold) was accredited to his court from the King of England, and the Nawab claimed to be an independent sovereign in direct alliance with his Britannic Majesty's Government, as different from the East India Company. It was only in February, 1787, that the military alliance, by which the Company undertook to maintain the troops and the Nawab to pay its subsidy, was concluded. But after the annihilation of Mysore power the necessity for maintaining a native state which should bear the burden of defence ceased to exist and the Carnatic was annexed.

Though Warren Hastings himself had laid it down that the basic principle of the Company's policy was 'the extension of the influence of the British nation without enlarging its circle of defence,' the subsidiary system, by which the Company insisted on every state in alliance maintaining a body of British troops at its expense, was a slow and gradual development. When the Maharajah of Travancore suggested at the time of Tipu's invasion that he may be supplied with a detachment of the Company's forces for which he was prepared to pay, the Madras

Government refused the request. Again, after the Mysore war, a like suggestion, when made by the Mahratta general to the Marquis of Cornwallis, met with disapproval. It was only in the time of the Marquis of Wellesley that a deliberate attempt was made to develop an Imperial polity based on the system of subsidiary alliance. Wellesley understood its implications and justly estimated its weakness, but came to the deliberate conclusion that under the existing circumstances of India, an indirect extension of sovereignty in this manner was to be preferred to a direct exercise of dominion. Wellesley brought under the operation of the subsidiary system, the Nizam, the Peishwa, Holkar, Scindia and temporarily the Rajputana states.

The history of these transactions may be briefly traced. The alliance with the Nizam dated from 1766. But as the power of the Company increased, the alliance underwent modifications, though not of so serious a nature as in the case of Oudh and the Carnatic. The Nizam was at the end of the century troubled by the exactions of the Mahrattas and wanted an alteration of the treaty of 1768, by which he was entitled to the support of British military forces. The explanatory letter which Lord Cornwallis gave to Meer Allum in 1789 extended the Sixth Article of the treaty into a stipulation that the force mentioned therein 'shall be furnished whenever the Nizam shall apply for it, provided it is not employed against any powers in alliance with the

Company.'[1] This letter of Lord Cornwallis was declared by a special resolution of Parliament, dated 15th March, 1792, to have the full force of a treaty executed in due form. Though this extended significance of the treaty gave it in appearance a military character, it was in practice clearly useless, as the British forces in the pay of the Nizam could not be used against the Mahrattas who were the only enemies then menacing him. This was soon made amply clear. The Mahratta confederacy under Parasuram Bhaw Patwardhan attacked the Nizam in 1795, and at Kurdla disaster overtook the Nizam's forces. The British alliance, which was the basis of his military power, was of no help, and Sir John Shore argued himself into the belief that a pacific policy was best suited to British prestige. The Nizam was temporarily turned into a tributary of the Peishwa, and he saw that the only way of shaking off that humiliating bond was to organise a standing force of his own under French commanders. The Earl of Mornington's new treaty enlarging the subsidiary force to six battalions, for which the Nizam was to pay a subsidy of 2,617,100 Rs., stipulated that the French force should be disbanded; and that, in case of differences between the Mahrattas and himself, the matter on his side would be referred to the Company. This important treaty, by which a permanent British force was stationed in the Nizam's territory and the French force disbanded, was put into operation by a masterful *coup d'état*. The

[1] Briggs, *Nizam*, vol. i. p. 252.

importance of the treaty lay not so much in the establishment of a permanent British force in the Hyderabad territories as in the surrender by the Nizam of his external independence. A separate and secret article of the treaty declared :

> No correspondence on affairs of importance shall in future on any account be carried on with the Sirkar of Rao Pandit Pradhan or with any of his dependents either by the Nawab Asaf Jah Bahadur or by the Hon'ble Company's Government without the mutual privity and consent of both contracting parties.

By this the Nizam ceased to be an independent ruler and his state took its place as the premier state in subordinate alliance with the British Government.

The same story is more or less repeated in the relations with the Mahrattas. By the famous Treaty of Bassein the Peishwa was also brought into the system of subsidiary alliance, by which the Mahratta State gave up its right of external sovereignty and undertook to maintain a British force in its territories. This treaty was strongly resented by the other members of the Mahratta confederacy, with the result that they and the Company entered into a struggle in which the genius of Wellington crushed the military prowess of Perron and his Mahratta confederates. By the Treaty of Sarje Anjegoan, Scindia's powers for offence were reduced, but the agreement was not in the nature of a subsidiary alliance. By the Treaty of Devagoan the Bhonsla Raja of Nagpur was brought into the system. The Treaty of Rajpur Ghat closed the war with Holkar, and the supremacy of the British arms was recognised over the whole of Central India. By the Treaty of Cambay in 1802 the Gaekwar of Baroda accepted the protection of the Company, and the campaign against Scindia and Holkar necessitated the alliance with Alwar and Bharatpur.

The first period of subordinate alliance may be said to close with this. It saw the rise of the Company from a position of equality into one of predominance. But the powers with whom the Company entered into alliance were equally independent states. Sometimes, as in the Marquis of Cornwallis's alliance against Tipu, the treaties were for specific purposes as between independent powers seeking a common objective. In other cases, as in the treaty with Alwar, it is for help in reducing a powerful enemy. But in all these treaties there are three important points which stand out :

(1) In the treaties between the Company and the States, there is a spirit of theoretical equality of status, and the States are recognised as being in the enjoyment of sovereign independence. The treaty with the Nizam and the Mahrattas, who were in theory and in fact in the enjoyment of absolute external and internal sovereignty, show a spirit of reciprocity. In the treaty with the Nizam, which was entered into for the purpose of taking 'means for the mutual defence of their respective possessions,' it is stated, 'whatever transactions, whether of great or small import, may in future take place between the aforesaid Rao Pandit Pradhan, or his

dependents, a *reciprocal* communication of the same shall be made to the other contracting party without delay and without reserve.'[1] Again, the preamble of the treaty of defensive alliance dated 12th October, 1800, mentions as the object of the treaty, 'the complete and *reciprocal protection* of their respective territories, together with those of their several allies and dependents.' It will also be of interest to note that up to 1829, the Governor-General, in his correspondence with the Nizam, used such terms as Niyaz Mund, which admitted an inferiority of rank, while the Nizam, speaking of himself, used the royal 'We.' It is not only in agreements with powerful rulers like the Nizam and the Peishwa that equality of status was recognised. In the treaty with the Rajah of Alwar, concluded during the campaign against the Mahratta chiefs, the Rajah is authorised to demand from the British Government aid 'if from the obstinacy of the opposite party no amicable terms can be reached,' which is a recognition of the rights of private and direct negotiations with other states.

(2) The second point which becomes clear is that the Company at that time had no intention of encroaching on the sovereignty of their allies and claiming for themselves the rights of an overlord. In fact, after the victories over Scindia Lord Wellesley wrote to the Secret Committee of the Court of Directors that the object of the Company should

[1] Separate article in the Treaty of Alliance, 1st of September, 1798, page 170, *Wellington Despatches*.

be security, and Scindia was given the option of coming into the defensive alliance or keeping out. The policy later on pursued of evolving a state system in which the British Company will stand as a paramount overlord over subordinate allies was absent even up to the last stages of Wellesley's rule. It would be seen that in the case of the Nizam or Scindia or any of the powers which came into the subsidiary alliance there was no limitation of the armies to be maintained by them.

(3) A third consideration is that by a most unequivocal declaration in the case of independent powers brought into the defensive system, the Company guaranteed them full and absolute sovereignty in their internal affairs. Every treaty with a state previously independent, or taken into alliance for help in campaigns, lays this down expressly. That the clause so laid down was no merely empty profession, but a legal obligation undertaken to respect the sovereign rights of the allies, is clear from the fact that Wellesley frankly recognised its 'baneful' effects and implications, and tried to remedy it wherever he could. In his despatch to the Court of Directors dated 3rd of August, 1799, regarding the treaty with Mysore, he wrote, 'In framing this engagement it was my determination to establish the most unqualified community of interests between the Government of Mysore and the Company. . . . Recollecting the inconveniences and embarrassments which have arisen to all parties concerned under the double Govern-

ments and conflicting authorities unfortunately established in Oudh, the Carnatic and Tanjore, I resolved to reserve to the Company the most extensive and indisputable rights of inter-position in the internal affairs of Mysore as well as an unlimited right of assuming direct management of the Country.'[1]

Arthur Wellesley, his eminent brother, also well realised the results that would follow the subsidiary system of treaties, and pointed them out forcibly in a memorandum. He remarked: 'The treaties of alliances had a stipulation "that the Native States should be independent in all the questions of its internal government, and at the very moment in which this stipulation was made the interference of the British Government was required."' If, therefore, after a full recognition of its weakness, Lord Wellesley had uniformly to guarantee this independence in treaties he made with Indian rulers, it is clear that political circumstances necessitated it and that the stipulation was made not merely to satisfy the pride of the rulers but as a contract meant to be fulfilled to the very letter.

But these treaties of mutual amity, friendly co-operation and reciprocal obligations, were soon to end. Their place in all future engagements was to be taken by treaties of subordinate co-operation, allegiance and loyalty. The position of the Company changed in ten years' time from being one of the powers of India into that of a paramount power, and in the treaties made after 1813, this became perfectly clear.

[1] *Wellesley Despatches*, lxxvii. and viii.

II

FROM THE MARQUIS OF HASTINGS TO THE MUTINY

Between the annexationists, whose cause was so ably presented by the future Duke of Wellington, and the non-interventionists, who controlled the policy of the Court of Directors, Lord Wellesley's system based on the maintenance of the *status quo* in subordinate alliance, with a view mainly to secure the Company's possessions from any kind of attack, found but few supporters. Most of the officials in India were thorough annexationists, while the statesmen of an earlier generation, represented by Cornwallis, Teignmouth and Barlow, stood out for non-intervention. Both these schools based their argument on the common ground that the subsidiary alliances created a system which gave additional responsibility to the Company without strengthening its position. Thus Arthur Wellesley said: 'By this system the authority of the native governments is paralysed, and they have invariably to resort to the assistance of the British Government for the management of their own internal concerns. In fact, it naturally amounted to setting up impotent rulers, who could be of no help in case of war but may be a considerable source of trouble if the defence of the Empire's frontier is dependent on them.' After Wellesley's departure, Barlow and Cornwallis attempted to reverse this policy and, in fact, the interlude was one in which some of Wellesley's treaties were dissolved and further commitments refused. In 1809 Lord Minto refused to enter into an alliance with Bhopal, and the treaty which Barlow negotiated with Holkar ceded to him Tonk and Rampoora and dissolved the treaty with Jeypore. By the treaty with Scindia at Mustaphapur the Government of India undertook not to enter into treaties with the Rajahs of Udaipur, Jhodpur and other tributaries of Scindia situated in Malwa, Mundar and Marwar, or to interfere with the settlement that Scindia may make with those chiefs. The idea was, as Metcalfe points out in his memorandum, to withdraw from all alliances and connections west of the Jumna, and though the force of circumstances prevented Lord Minto from adhering to it strictly, the policy of expansion was under an eclipse until the time of the Earl Moira, later known as the Marquis of Hastings. There are exceptions of far-reaching importance in the treaties with the Cis-Sutlej states of Patiala, Nabha and Jind. These states had made friends with the Mahrattas as against the growing power of Maharajah Ranjit Singh. But after the defeat of Holkar their position became precarious. Disputes among the Phulkian rulers gave an opportunity for Ranjit Singh to intervene. It was as a result of that ambitious king's encroachments that the chiefs approached the British Government for a treaty of alliance. The British Government intervened to secure the states from annexation, and by a proclamation took the Sutlej area under its protection.

In the Marquis of Hastings, the Anglo-Indian advocates of *real politik* who talked about the 'proud pre-eminence' of the British nation, found an avowed champion. The Mahratta and Pindari wars and the settlement that followed rendered the Cornwallis-Minto period a time of respite and continued the policy and elaborated the principles which had guided Marquis Wellesley. The feudatory system, which I distinguish from the system of protected alliances, came into existence with the changed condition which after the complete destruction of Mahratta power placed the Company in a position of unquestioned supremacy in India. All the treaties made in this period with the smaller chiefs are of a nature different from the reciprocal treaties of mutual goodwill and reciprocal obligations entered into with the Nizam, Scindia and other powers of the earlier period. The Company stood no longer in need of help from the minor states, and the treaties were negotiated not for *the security* of the Company's dominions as in most cases up to the end of Wellesley's time, but for the purpose of extending the benefits of *pax britannica* and asserting the pre-eminent authority of the British. The treaties with the Rajputana States, which brought the whole of that area under British sovereignty, were hardly in the nature of reciprocal obligations. In most of these treaties, the rights of protection, and the full authority of arbitration, and the complete subordination of the ruler are clearly laid down.

The same is the case with Central India. No less than one hundred and forty-five rulers were recognised, but their position was distinctly subordinate. Though still declared independent in internal affairs, these states were declared to be in complete subordination to the Government of India which, as a broad line of settlement, accepted the autonomy of these chiefs. What is to be borne in mind is that in Bundlekund, and later in Kathiawad, it was not from individual treaties, each arising from different conditions and each negotiated with guarantees of rights that the rulers derived their authority, but on the basis of general political settlement which accepted the feudatory system prevalent in these areas. Only three states, Orcha, Datia and Samthar, are bound by formal treaties ; the rest are confirmed in their possession by sanads, grants and ikrar namahs. It is clear enough that these states stand altogether on a different footing from states like Gwalior, Hyderabad, Travancore, Baroda and the Phulkian States with which the Company allied itself on specific and definite conditions.

The facts with regard to the Kathiawad chieftains will explain this position better. The British rights of sovereignty in Kathiawad are based not on treaty with those states directly but on agreement concluded with the Gaekwar. It states, 'With the view of promoting the prosperity, peace and safety of the country and in order that the Gaekwar's government shall receive without trouble and with facility the amount of tribute due to it from the Provinces of Kathiawad and Mahee Kanta, it has been arranged with the British Government that His Highness Sayaji Roa Gaekwar shall not send his troops into the districts belonging to the Zamindars of both the provinces without the consent of the Company's government; and shall not prefer any claims against the Zamindars or others in those provinces except through the arbitration of the Company's government.'

The 'States' and jurisdictions thus brought under the British sway enjoyed no sovereign rights, though their privileges and honours were assured to them. The British Government merely took over the sovereign rights that the Gaekwar and the Peishwa exercised on these chiefs, and has continued to maintain them as a separate class which is no more that of the ruling princes than it is of ordinary subjects. The engagements made with these states are generally on one pattern. They declare that the territory was received by cession from the Peishwa and *annexed* to the British dominions, but that the states of the chiefs are continued to them out of motives of justice, benevolence and good faith; they bind the chiefs to implicit submission, loyalty and attachment to the British Government. They are liable to such control as the British Government may see fit to exercise and the rights and powers of the chiefs are limited to those that have been expressly conferred.[1]

The other states which came into the protection of the Company's government after the Marquis of Hastings' time stand also on a different footing. The minor states of the Punjab, Chamba, Veanda and Suket were granted terms which rendered them feudatories and implied specific limitations on their rights. Kashmir, it will be remembered, was sold in sovereignty to Gulab Singh, but on condition that succession should be to his *heirs in the male line*. In this case evidently the clause was introduced to give the British Government the definite right of determining succession.

With the extension of the system to the Punjab States, it can be said that thc policy of protected and subordinate alliance reached its fullest limit. Very few states have since been added to the polity that developed, and whatever was added, was by special grace, as in the case of Benares, which was constituted into a ruling state by Lord Minto's government or under the special circumstance of the military policy pursued in the North-Western frontier, as in the case of Dir and Chitral. It has already been noticed how the earlier treaties up to 1813 differed materially in the nature of the relations and in the position, power and independence guaranteed to the states. The treaties with them were in fact and not only in theory treaties of alliance.

[1] See note on Kathiawad chiefs at the end of the book : Appendix I ; Aitchison, vol. v. p. 17.

They were entered into for the purpose of the security of British frontiers and were more in the nature of an allied defensive system. The treaties made from the time of the Marquis of Hastings were in the nature of authority given by special favour and naturally were of a subordinate character. This difference was recognised then, mainly in questions relating to succession, annexation and the exercise of sovereign rights, as will be shown later.

The Governor-Generalship of Dalhousie, which marks an epoch in the history of British India, is important from the point of view of Indian state history only for the growth of political principles which we shall have to discuss in detail later on. He claimed for the Government feudal and sovereign rights over the petty states which the British Company had itself set up, and rigorously applied the principle of lapse and escheat for the purpose of annexing the dominions of minor principalities. The difference in the nature of states and the altered basis of the new treaties were fully recognised by Dalhousie, and his attempt was mainly to sweep away from the board the minor princes and Jagirdars whom a senseless policy had propped up. Sir Charles Metcalfe in 1837 classified the Indian states into quasi-sovereign states and dependent principalities, treaty princes and Sanad chiefs, and it was on this classification that Dalhousie based his policy. With regard to those who derived their authority from the government of the Company, Dalhousie followed a policy of constructive feudalism, applying the principle of lapse, escheat, control and annexation. The rulers of Satara, Jhansi, Tanjore and Jaitpur can only be considered in a different light from the Nizam, or Scindia, or any other of the treaty princes. The Satara Raj was practically created in 1819 by the British Government; but the case of Oudh and Berar are slightly different. Oudh was not annexed on the ground of lapse or escheat, but of *misgovernment*, and it is clear that in the case of a treaty state such an action would have been illegal and highly arbitrary. But Oudh, though its rulers enjoyed the regal dignity, was even worse than a vassal state. From the time of Warren Hastings the authority of the Oudh rulers had practically disappeared. So early as the time of Wellesley Oudh had ceased to have even the vestiges of independence, and the Company for all practical purposes treated it as a part of its own territories. Its annexation has no definite bearing on the policy pursued towards states with guaranteed independence, though the Marquis of Dalhousie's action in this case was arbitrary, harsh and altogether indefensible, and based on the most unjustifiable fraud committed by Lord Auckland, who refused to announce to the King of Oudh the abrogation of the treaty by which that ruler had signed away important rights. To a large extent the annexation of Oudh and the discreditable character of the negotiations were the reason for the deep-seated unrest which found vent in the Sepoy Mutiny.

Besides these acts of annexation the Marquis of Dalhousie's rule is important in the elaboration of principles which we shall have to discuss in connection with the rights of sovereign power.

The effect of this system of 'independent' rule by rajas and nawabs, whose power was guaranteed, but in whose administration no interest was taken by the supreme Government, was most deplorable. Before the alliance with the Company, these states were forced by circumstances to maintain efficiency of administration, as otherwise they would be swallowed by their powerful neighbours. They had to be economical, as otherwise the treasury would be empty when the enemy approached. They had to cultivate the goodwill of their subjects, as otherwise internal rebellion would give their enemies the best chance of conquest. With the British alliance and the security that followed thereafter all these circumstances which checked the vices of irresponsible autocracy disappeared. The courts of these princes became the theatre of the most degraded debauchery and the most horrible misgovernment. Successive British administrators and diplomatists noted this fact with some surprise. Marquis Wellesley himself recognised this, and he makes it clear in his Despatch to the Court of Directors on the Treaty of Mysore. Wellington in a celebrated minute discussed with surprising acumen the results of this policy, which he said, 'paralysed the native ruler, and made him dependent entirely on British support.' Writing on the subsidiary force and the political system based on it, after Wellesley's policy had worked for over fifteen years, Sir Thomas Munro, a great and venerated name in British Indian history, said:

> It has the natural tendency to render the Government of every country in which it exists, weak and oppressive; to extinguish all honourable spirit among the higher classes of society, to degrade and impoverish the whole people. The usual remedy of a bad Government in India is a quiet revolution in the palace, or a violent one by rebellion. But the presence of the British Force cuts off every chance of remedy by supporting the Prince on the throne against any foreign and domestic enemy. It renders him indolent by teaching him to trust to strangers for his security; cruel and avaricious by showing him that he has nothing to fear from the hatred of his subjects. Wherever the subsidiary system is introduced, the country will soon bear the marks of it, in decaying villages, a decreasing population. This has long been observed in the Dominions of the Peishwa and the Nizam.[1]

Lord Cornwallis writing to Lord Lake on 30th August, 1805, remarked on the same phenomenon. 'From reports I have received from the residents,' said the Marquis, 'I am sorry to find that the States who are most intimately connected with us are reduced to the most forlorn condition; that these powers possess no funds or troops on which they can depend; that anarchy and disaffection prevail universally throughout the dominions, and that unless the British Governments exercised a power and an ascendancy that they ought not to

[1] *Wellesley Despatches*, Appendix.

exert those Governments would be immediately dissolved.'

The history of Indian states during the first half of the nineteenth century when the full effects of the subsidiary system began to manifest themselves is a strange and illuminating, if sad, commentary on this text. The Nizam's administration during the long reign of Sicunder Jah proved a standing testimony to the blighting effects of this system. Affairs fell into such disorder that the Nizam, aided by his corrupt ministers, seemed to be following the disastrous path of the nawabs of Arcot. The administration was much in debt to Palmer and Company, and the whole system of government had broken down, resulting at one time in the appointment of British Commissioners for the Provinces. It was only the genius, tact and diplomatic ability of Salar Jung that saved the state from annexation and ruin. The case of Oudh is notorious, and requires no elaboration. The history of Scindia's dominions from the Treaty of Mustafanager to the Mutiny is one of progressive decline, leading in some cases to military revolts and rebellions. The case of Holkar is more disgraceful. The administration of Maharajah Hari Rao became so unbearable that in 1835 his subjects besieged him in his palace and tried to assassinate him. Anand Rao Gaekwar's administration repeated the same sad story. After Anand Rao's death the financial and administrative position of the state became much more scandalous and the Gaekwar was unable to pay his debts to private creditors. In Travancore, the Resident, Colonel Munro, had to take up the administration of the state, and the proposal was actually made for the annexation of Cochin on the ground of extreme maladministration. In Mysore matters went much further. A committee was appointed in 1830 to enquire into the state of affairs, and the administration of Mysore had to be taken over by the Government.

Thus in every state which had come under the subsidiary alliance, its influence led to an utter and complete breakdown of the Indian system of government. The responsibility for this lay almost entirely on the British authorities. Matters had come to such a scandalous state that the London *Times* in a remarkable leading article described the situation thus in 1853 :[1]

> We have emancipated these pale and ineffectual pageants of royalty from the ordinary fate that awaits on an oriental despotism. . . . This advantage (of securing able and vigorous princes through rebellion) we have taken away from the inhabitants of the States of India still governed by Native Princes. It has been well said that we give these Princes power without responsibility. Our hand of iron maintains them on the throne, despite their imbecility, their vices and their crimes. The result is in most of the states, a chronic anarchy, under which the revenues of the states are dissipated between the mercenaries of the camp and the minions of the Court. The heavy and arbitrary taxes levied on the miserable raiyats serve only to feed the meanest and the most degraded of mankind.

[1] Quoted in Arnold : *Marquis of Dalhousie*, vol. ii. pp. 2-84.

> The theory seems in fact admitted that the Government is not for the people but the people for the King, and that so long as we secure the King his sinecure royalty, we discharge all the duty that we, as Sovereigns of India, owe to his subjects who are virtually ours.

This vigorous characterisation of the conditions prevalent in the states, and the fundamental cause of it, was not in the least exaggerated. The great danger to British power at the time of the Mutiny was the unsettled state of the country administered by the Indian rulers. The soldiery of the Maharajah Scindia was in open revolt, and the military establishment of Holkar was in a dangerous state of ferment. The short-sightedness of the policy pursued towards the states between 1813-1855 became clear in the blazing light of the conflagration of 1857. Then it became evident that it was not sufficient for the British Company to go on claiming sovereign rights and annexing states, but it had also to maintain and guarantee the rights and just authority of the rulers, and that even those whose rights and dignities have been conferred by sanads and grants should be treated with greater consideration. The settlement that followed the 'Mutiny' marks the end of the second chapter in the history of the British relations with Indian states, when on the basis of the differentiation between independent and dependent rulers the Company tried to evolve, so far as the latter was concerned, a system of public law based on what may be called feudal rights. In the first half of that period a large number of these states, mainly in Kathiawad and Bundlekund were created, and in the latter half a definite attempt was made to apply to them the principles of law and rights taken by analogy from the feudal law of Europe.[1] The failure of that part of the policy is written in letters of blood in the story of the Indian 'Mutiny,' and, learning their lessons from it, the British authorities wisely gave up as impracticable the policy that had led to the annexation of Satara, Jhansi, Tanjore and other minor states.

[1] See chap. iv. and Appendix, Note I.

III

THE CROWN

THE great Mutiny and the subsequent assumption of direct sovereignty by the Crown changed the whole historical and constitutional position of the Indian rulers. From the foreign and independent allies of a sovereign corporation, the great states found themselves transformed into the protected 'feudatories' of the Crown of England, whose sovereignty over them was boldly and frankly announced and pressed with the unquestioned authority of irresistible military power. Lord Canning himself declared in 1862 that 'the Crown of England stood forward the unquestioned ruler and paramount power in all India, and was for the first time brought face to face with the *feudatories*, and that there was a reality in the suzerainty of the Sovereign of England which never existed before and which was eagerly acknowledged by the Chiefs.' The logical implications of this change and its far-reaching influence upon the development of Indian polity will occupy the succeeding chapters. From the point of view of the historical background the important facts of this period may be noted here.

In taking over the Company's territories for direct administration under the Crown, the Indian rulers were especially assured that the treaty rights and obligations of the states were in no way affected. The Government of India Act of 1858 contained as its last clause the provision that 'all treaties made by the Company shall be binding on Her Majesty.' The historic proclamation of the Queen put the position more elaborately :

> We hereby announce to the Native Princes of India that all treaties and engagements made with them by or under the authority of the Hon'ble East India Company are by us accepted and will be scrupulously maintained, and we look for the like observance on their part.
>
> We desire no extension of our present territorial possessions, and while we will permit no aggression upon our dominions or our rights to be attempted with impunity, we shall sanction no encroachment on those of others. We shall respect the rights, the dignity and honour of Native Princes as our own ; and we desire that they, as well as their own subjects, should enjoy that prosperity and that social advancement which can only be secured by internal peace and good government.

This was acceptance in full of the obligations and engagements of the Company, and though in appearance it was a pacific continuation of the old system, it effected a remarkable if a silent revolution. In the immediate relation between the states and the British power, the changes affected by the Mutiny were of importance. All the Indian rulers had remained firm, and indubitably it was their attitude that turned the scales in the campaign.

The Maharajah of Jind personally took part in the attack on Delhi, and the firm resolution of Salar Jung prevented the extension of the conflagration to the south. Naturally, after the pacification, the states which took direct and prominent part in helping the British authorities were rewarded by the grant of large territories. More than this, the policy enunciated in 1841 of 'abandoning no just and honourable accession of territory or revenue,' which, in plain language, meant the policy of annexation on any possible pretext, was reversed. The British Government definitely and deliberately laid it down as a principle for their own conduct that annexation of territories as a solution either of the problem of misgovernment, disloyalty of the ruler, or for strategic considerations, should be ruled out. As a consequence there developed a new policy, which accepted the moral responsibility of the British Government for a minimum of good government, security, law and order within the territories of the Indian states. Speaking to an assemblage of Rajput princes, Lord Mayo, in whose time the foundations of the new policy were laid, thus expressed the general principles that the Government of India had accepted for the guidance of its political conduct. 'If we support you in your power, we expect in return good government. We demand that everywhere through the length and breadth of Rajputana, justice and order shall prevail; that every man's property shall be secure; that the traveller shall come and go in safety; that the cultivator shall enjoy the fruits of his labour, and the trader the produce of his commerce ; that you shall make roads and undertake the construction of those works of irrigation which will improve the condition of the people and swell the revenues of your states ; that you shall encourage education and provide for the relief of the sick.'

That this policy involved the practice of veiled intervention, and an effective reduction of the constitutional position of the princes and their conversion into dependent states, will be made clear in the succeeding pages. If it definitely put a stop to annexations it introduced in its stead rule by loaned officers, by nominated dewans, and strict control through the Residents. The attempt was to aggrandise not the territories but the power of the Central Government, and to make the Indian states integral portions of the Indian polity.

This policy was based on the legal theory that the rights of the Moghul emperor had accrued to the British as a result of the displacement of the Padshah at Delhi following the Mutiny. The British Crown claimed to stand forth not only in the place of the East India Company, with whom many of the states had had treaties on the basis of equality, but put on itself the decayed mantle of the Moghul Empire, and claimed the rights of sovereignty which Akbar and Shah Jehan had enforced. This theory found a pompous expression in the title of Kaiser i Hind assumed by the Queen in 1876, immediately after the death of Bahadur Shah, the last Indian sovereign who sat on the throne of Delhi. To enforce this, a Durbar was held in Delhi, which Lord Hartington declared to be the assumption of the fallen estate of the Moghul emperors. To this Durbar all Indian states were invited, and in effect forced, to attend. The Nizam, to whom the Governor-General up to 1829 wrote in terms of humility, and with whom the treaty was made on terms of equality; Scindia, whose alliance left him independent ruler of his state with obligations on a reciprocal basis; Travancore, whose Maharajah was an ally of the Company before it ever acquired even dewany rights, were forced to attend the Durbar at Delhi, and to realise that their position was constitutionally altered and that they bore allegiance to the Empress, equally with the one hundred and eighty-seven chiefs of Kathiawad and the other new creations of British policy. Against this claim by the Crown, the Nizam and other important rulers strongly protested as a lowering of their dignity and an encroachment on their sovereignty. But before the might of Britain they had to stoop, and the imagination of Lord Lytton and the love of colour and extravagance of Disraeli were satisfied with the pomp and pageantry of an assemblage of princes such as the world had never seen before. The Indian states, whatever their previous status was, were now brought unmistakably under the supreme authority of the British Crown, and were practically forced to abandon for the time at least the claims of sovereignty and treatment according to treaty.

Lord Lytton's other proposals included an Indian peerage, a privy council of princes and durbars at regular intervals. This policy was much resented by the princes, and was as a result abandoned by the Government in its more elaborate forms.

But the relations underwent a subtle change. The theory was laid down that as against the 'paramount power' the treaty states had no 'rights,' that all their privileges, status, rank, dignities and jurisdictions were dependent on the goodwill of the King. '*The Sovereignty* of the Crown is everywhere unchallenged,' said Lord Curzon in his speech at the Bhawalpur installation.[1] 'It has itself laid down the limitations of its own prerogative.' This view was first promulgated in 1860, when Lord Canning declared that 'the territories under the sovereignty of the Crown became at once as important and as integral a part of India as territories under its direct domination. Together they form one direct care, and the political system which the Moghuls had not completed and the Mahrattas never contemplated is now an established fact of history.'[2] But in establishing that political system, which the Moghuls never completed and the Mahrattas never contemplated, Great Britain had to ride rough-shod over treaties, and had to forget rights and obligations and deny validity to undertakings most solemnly entered into in the hour of her need. Rights and prerogatives never claimed by the Company and

[1] *Lord Curzon in India*, p. 227.

[2] *Imperial Gazetteer*, vol. iv. p. 82.

never conceded by the Indian rulers have been exercised on the general claim of succession to Moghul pretensions. The list of obligations which, irrespective of their treaties have, says Lee Warner, devolved on the native states through the channel of royal prerogative, includes the right of the Queen's Viceroy to recognise successions, to assume the guardianship of minor princes, to confer or withdraw titles, decorations and salutes, to sanction the acceptance of foreign orders, to grant passports and to recognise or appoint consular officers. Those encroachments on the legitimate rights of Indian states, based on the theory of the British Crown being the apostolic successor or testamentary heir of the Moghuls, constitute the chief characteristic of the relations between Indian states and the Empire during the period after the Mutiny. In the succeeding chapters we shall study its growth in all its aspects.

This much must be noted here. The feudatory character of the states was emphasised by various viceroys. The policy of Imperial Durbars inaugurated by Lord Lytton was continued by Lord Curzon and Lord Hardinge, and on each of these occasions emphasis was laid on the allegiance to the British Crown which is demanded of the Indian rulers. That the minor princes of India have accepted this without grudge can be seen by the utterances of chiefs like the Jam Sahib of Nawanagar who, in his speech at the Princes' Conference, spoke all through of his loyalty to his King. The chiefs of Kathiawad, as has been pointed out, stand on a different footing from the rulers with whom the Company had direct treaties of reciprocal alliance like Gwalior, Hyderabad and Travancore; but the tendency has been to forget their essential difference and to establish a uniformity of political practice which classed the descendant of Asaf Jah with that of Amir Khan, and Scindia with the petty chief of a few square miles in Kathiawad.

This policy of assuming sovereign rights over the states and the conversion of their rulers from semi-independent allies to feudatories, definitely failed in the case of Nepal and Afghanistan. In 1877 the Amir of Afghanistan and the Prime Minister of Nepal were invited to the Durbar, and both politely declined the invitation. Sir James Stephen, who was law member in the Viceroy's Cabinet, wrote that 'Chiefs like the Amir of Kabul must be dealt with on the understanding that they occupy a distinctly inferior position.' Till 1919 there was an attempt to treat Afghanistan as a native state in an inferior grade of relationship. Afghanistan was allowed to have a representative at the Viceregal Court alone, and its ruler was not styled His Majesty; and by arrangement with Russia its foreign relations had to be conducted through the Indian Foreign Office. The case of Nepal was similar. Ever since the Treaty of Sagauli, 1816, a British Resident lived at Khatmandu, but the sagacious policy of the Prime-Ministerial family steadily resisted the attempted inclusion of Nepal in the British political system, so that now she has been recognised as a completely independent sovereign state, and the Resident has been transformed into the British Envoy to the court of His Majesty the King of Nepal.

If this policy of absorption has failed in relation to Afghanistan and Nepal, it has been successful in all other directions. Kashmir was brought definitely within the system, and the Khan of Khelat lost his independence and became a protected ruler. On the frontier tribal chieftains are now being converted by slow degrees into territorial rulers with salutes, orders and dignities, and a new province with a number of princes like the Nawab of Dir has been created. Elsewhere there was no increase in the number of states, with the single and significant exception of the Maharajah of Benares, who was converted from a landed magnate into a ruling prince, perhaps as a tardy compensation for the historic wrong done by Hastings to Chet Singh.

But other changes of an important constitutional character, showing that the relations between the states and the government are still undergoing change, have taken place during the last eight years. The delegation of an Indian ruler to represent the princes at the peace negotiations, the constitution of the Princes' Chamber, the representation of the princes at the Imperial Conference, and more than all, the declared policy of the Government to surrender some of the rights that it had so far claimed are evidences of an unseen revolution in political relations, the facts, tendencies, and implications whereof deserve thorough study.

IV

THE GROWTH OF CENTRAL POWER

THE encroachment of a strong central power over the rights of those in loose alliance with it is one of the most fundamental facts in the history of states. The tendency of the major partner to swallow by slow degrees its minor associates and allies is writ large wherever federalism or even confederacy has been tried. The confederacy of Delos was transformed in course of time into the Athenian empire. When in face of the Persian enemy united resistance on the part of the minor Greek states was first organised under the leadership of Athens, the principle adopted was one of equality of status among the constituent members. But the alliance was turned into an empire, and Athens became the 'paramount power' in the language of Anglo-Indian historians, and the cities and states in alliance became subordinate associates. The following description by a learned historian of Greece shows the change that came over the political system that started like the British Indian Empire in its relations with Indian states through military alliances, and ended in the establishment of sovereignty. 'There was no hard and fast system. Each city had its own individual arrangement, its own measure of restricted autonomy. The closer dependence of these tributary states on Athens was in many cases marked by the presence of Athenian civil officers. But there was one obligation which was common to all, the obligation of furnishing soldiers to the League in time of war.' [1]

The same tendency is illustrated in the constitutional relations between England and Scotland. The Treaty of Union of 1707 which created the kingdom of Great Britain, guaranteed for the northern kingdom certain definite rights and privileges, some of which have now disappeared. Scotland has preserved the identity of her national existence in some ways, but the encroachments of the central government have been well marked and important.

Probably the tendency of central authority to expand at the expense of its constituent members is best illustrated in the history of the United States of America. It is well known that when the federal state was first constituted the thirteen states that signed the Union considered themselves entirely independent of each other except for the purposes specifically laid down. Jefferson desired to confine federal action to the conduct of foreign affairs, and even Hamilton, of whom it was said by Talleyrand that having never seen Europe he had divined it, did not seek its indefinite expansion. All the great institutions of the United States, especially

[1] Bury, *History of Greece*, Macmillan, 1902, p. 339.

the Senate and the Federal Court, are constituted with a view to maintain the independence of the states and guarantee them from the encroachment of central power. And yet, what has been the result? During the course of the half century that followed the death of Jefferson, the independent and co-ordinate power of the states was practically annihilated, and the authority of the central government extended on all sides. It was also discovered, says the historian of American democracy, 'that there are unforeseen directions, such as questions relating to Banking, Currency, internal communications, through which the federal power can strengthen its hold on the nation.'[1]

The same tendencies are to be observed in the case of Germany, and perhaps in a more accentuated form. When the Reich was founded the greatest care was taken to maintain intact the sovereign power of some of the chief states, for nowhere was particularism more strongly marked or enshrined in hoary traditions of dynastic history than in the territories ruled by the Wittelsbachs. Many of the important features of the constitution that Bismarck framed were intended to make Bavaria, Saxony and other independent states feel that in finding a greater unity they were not losing their own independence. But how has this constitution worked? As Treitschke points out, the Imperial constitution soon showed itself to be unitary in all but name. The criminal law of the Empire has been made uniform

[1] Bryce, *American Commonwealth*, vol. ii. p. 8.

and enforced under the authority of the central government. All German troops swear allegiance to the Reich, and railway management posts and telegraphs and communications bearing on imperial defence are vested in the Bundesrath. After the war the authority of the central government has advanced much further as dynastic particularism has vanished at least for the time.

In India the assertion of central authority over the states has in some degree been more marked and has shown a tendency on the part of the Imperial authorities to decide doubtful points in their own favour. The main lines in which this authority advanced without being noticed by the public were in the railway, postal and telegraphic systems, educational policy as controlled by universities, extra-territorial jurisdiction as regards Europeans, the displacement of separate coinage and the vague assumption of legal claims about deposition, sanction for succession, right to give titles, etc. In every new development, either in transport facilities, banking, or military services, the vigilant British Government has put forward its own claims, which the princes, unable to discuss them or to come to an agreement among themselves, have been incapable of resisting. Lord Chelmsford himself, in his speech to the Princes' Conference, declared :

> There is no doubt that with the growth of new conditions and the unification of India under the British power political doctrines have constantly developed. In the case of extra-territorial jurisdiction, railway and telegraph

> construction, limitation of armaments, coinage, currency and opium policy and the administration of cantonments, to give some of the more salient instances, the relations between the States and the Imperial Government have been changed. The change, however, has come about in the interests of India as a whole. . . We cannot deny, however, that the treaty position has been affected and that a body of usages in some cases arbitrary but always benevolent has come into being.[1]

The legal bases of the policy of encroachment which have converted the Indian states into an integral part of the imperial polity have been mainly royal prerogatives, implications of treaty rights and strategical considerations. Besides these three main grounds the Government has enunciated and carried out a policy of direct intervention in the states on any and every matter on the claim that the protection which the Government affords entitles it, whatever the clauses of treaties might be, to guarantee the people of the states a minimum of good government. The letter of Lord Reading to the premier Indian ruler dated so late as 22nd March, 1926, put forward this point of view in a most unequivocal manner :

> The sovereignty of the Crown is supreme in India. . . . Its supremacy is not based only upon treaties and engagements, but exists independently of them, and quite apart from its prerogative in matters relating to foreign power and policies, it is the right and duty of the British Government, while scrupulously respecting all treaties and engagements, to preserve peace and good order throughout India. The consequences that follow are so well known

[1] *Lord Chelmsford's Speeches*, vol. ii. p. 278.

> and so clearly apply no less to your Exalted Highness than to other rulers that it seems hardly necessary to point them out. But if illustrations are necessary, I would remind your Exalted Highness that the Ruler of Hyderabad along with other rulers received in 1862 a sanad declaratory of the British Government's desire for the perpetuation of his house and government subject to continued loyalty to the Crown; that no succession to the musnad of Hyderabad is valid unless it is recognised by H.M. the King Emperor; and that the British Government is the only arbiter in case of disputed succession.
>
> The right of the British Government to intervene in internal affairs of Indian States is another instance of the consequences necessarily involved in the supremacy of the British Crown. . . . Where Imperial interests are concerned or the general welfare of the people of a state is seriously and grievously affected by the action of its government, it is with the paramount power that the ultimate necessity for taking remedial action, if necessary, must lie.

It must be noticed, however, that there no definite or uniform code of political practice is followed by the Government of India in this matter. Bureaucracy has a special tendency to systematise things to suit habits of work based on rulings and precedents, and therefore in this direction also an attempt has been made, as Lord Curzon openly declared, to conform to one type. This attempt to bring the treaty states and petty principalities into one category, which found public expression in the three Delhi Durbars, had two effects. It reduced the independent states to complete subordination and the status of allegiance, and it raised the minor principalities to a higher status. Practice appropriate in the case of lesser chiefs, said the Montagu-Chelmsford report, was inadvertently applied to the greater ones also. When the question was raised at the Chiefs' Conference of differentiating between sovereign princes and vassal chiefs, previous practice, irrespective of treaty provisions, was found to be a great difficulty, and Lord Chelmsford confessed that as matters stood now differentiation would be impracticable, and agreed finally that as treaty relations had changed, the salute list, however arbitrary and meaningless, was the only possible basis of distinction.

The unforeseen directions in which the central power has consolidated itself at the expense of Indian states have been to a large extent due to the direct and constructive interpretation of treaties by the political department. In this the sovereign power has been governed by considerations of its own claims as sovereign of the whole of India, a claim definitely and unhesitatingly put forward by Viceroys from Canning to Curzon, by its own international obligations towards other powers, such as in the case of extradition, suppression of drug traffic, economic and fiscal expediency, and military defence. In international relations, India must necessarily be treated as a unit, and the extension of the authority of the paramount power, especially as all treaties uniformly surrender their external independence and the right of separate negotiations, cannot be questioned. But even here the collective action of Indian princes has led recently to considerable change in their status, and the presence of a representative of Indian princes on the war cabinet and in the Imperial conferences has inaugurated an era in which, having surrendered their rights of negotiations and independent representation, they have gained the benefits of wider partnership.

V

SOVEREIGN RIGHTS

EVEN before the Company was formally dissolved and the Crown undertook the direct government of India, there had developed in the relations between the paramount power and the states certain definite rights of sovereignty. The statesmen of the Company made, however, a clear distinction between the dependent vassal states and the independent treaty states. Wellesley recognised this difference in his despatch justifying the treaty with the restored family in Mysore. In 1837 Sir Charles Metcalfe emphasised this distinction, and the whole of the Marquis of Dalhousie's policy was based on it. Dalhousie claimed that the Crown had feudal rights over those petty principalities, like Satara, Jhansi and others, which had been created by the Company and stood on a different footing from states like Hyderabad, Gwalior and Travancore, which had definite treaty relations. His doctrine of lapse, escheat and other claims involving sovereign rights on the part of the Company affected only those petty principalities which could not, either historically or by virtue of authority enjoyed, claim to be more than feudatories. Over these the sovereignty of the

British power was asserted. An attempt was even made to extend the theory by claiming the right to refuse recognition to adoptions, and to depose and confiscate. But both the Court of Directors and the Marquis of Dalhousie emphasised the distinction between independent and vassal states. Sir William Wilson Hunter, after 'carefully reading the official correspondence,' states :

> Practically Lord Dalhousie classified the native states of India into two divisions. First, the sovereign or quasi-sovereign states, dating from the time of the Moghul Empire, or from a still earlier period, or from the period immediately following its dissolution. Second, the dependent native states which we had ourselves created in subordinate relations to the British Government. The first class included not only the great Mohammedan, Rajput and Mahratta States, but also in Lord Dalhousie's opinion states of small area if they had the claim of antiquity in favour of their semi-independence.

This useful and indeed historical distinction was, however, forgotten in the search for uniformity of practice. Lord Curzon declared that the Indian states represent 'a series of relationships that have grown up between the Crown and the Indian Princes under widely differing historical conditions but which in process of time *have conformed to a single type*.'[1]

Lord Chelmsford frankly admitted that 'practice appropriate in the case of lesser chiefs was inadvertently applied to the greater ones also.' It is

[1] *Lord Curzon in India*, p. 227.

here that the Indian princes have lost their treaty rights and have felt justly aggrieved at the interference of the British Government.

The rights claimed by the Government but never fully accepted by the states on the basis of sovereignty are what may be conveniently called feudal, for lack of a more exact term. They involve the right to settle succession, constitute regency, decree deposition, assume wardship (involving education), to constitute regency, recognise, limit and grant titles and permit adoption. In the case of dependent states the East India Company enforced every one of these, and the discontent created by its rapid application was one of the undoubted causes of the great rebellion.

The question of settling successions is one that is bound up historically with the growth of the East India Company. The first political interference of the Company in Arcot was in a succession dispute, and Mahommed Ali assumed the Suba with the permission and under the patronage of the Company. In Oudh, Sir John Shore, who claimed to adhere strictly to the principle of non-intervention, exercised the right of deciding who was the lawful heir as Warren Hastings and his council had done before him. Even in the case of the Mahrattas the cause of the series of wars with the Peishwa up to the Treaty of Bassein was the question of the succession of Raghoba. In 1803 Secunder Jah's succession was formally confirmed by the Emperor at Delhi, and the Company and, later on, the Crown as the inheritor of the Moghul traditions, claimed and enforced this right.

It must, however, be recognised that the policy of the Government of India on this matter has not been uniform. With regard to the larger and fully-powered states, the earlier policy was to leave to the ruler the full authority to determine succession. In 1826 when Dowlut Rao Scindia was lying ill, the Government of India urged him to adopt a successor, and wrote that 'nothing could be further from the wish and intention of the British Government than to exercise now and hereafter any intervention in the internal administration of his (Scindia's) country, that it did not pretend to any right to control or regulate succession to the State of Gwalior and that the Maharajah as the absolute ruler of the country should be considered to possess the undoubted right of determining the succession.'[1] The right to intervene in case of the princes set up by the British Government and standing in clearly subordinate relation to it was asserted by Sir Charles Metcalfe in 1837 on the application of the Rajah of Orcha for the recognition of his adopted heir. 'There is a wide difference in the disposal of the question between sovereign princes and jaghirdars, between those in possession of hereditary sovereignty in their own right and those who hold by grant from a sovereign a paramount power.'

In the despatch of the Secretary of State dated 24th July, 1891, the Cabinet of the Marquis of

[1] See again the Bhawalpur Case, p. 398, Aitchison, vol. viii.

Salisbury laid it down that 'it is admittedly the right and duty of Government to settle successions in protected States of India generally.' The Government of India, in a communication to the Home Government, had also laid it down as a principle fully understood and invariably applied in India 'that every succession must be recognised by the British Government and no succession is valid until such consent has been given.' In a letter addressed to the Chief Commissioner of the Central Provinces and published in the *Government of India Gazette*, it was laid down, 'I am to observe that succession to a native state is invalid until it receives in some form the sanction of the British authorities. Consequently an *ad interim* and unauthorised ceremony, carried out by the people of the state, cannot be recognised.'

Closely connected with this right of confirming succession is the right to permit or disallow adoption. The doctrine of lapse, based on the right of the paramount power to refuse permission to the adopted son succeeding to the public position as against the private properties of the ruler, has now been repudiated by the Government. But even when it was enforced the Company was careful to distinguish between dependent and independent rulers, and to claim the right only as against the former. The most important cases are those of Satara and Jhansi. Both of these, though principalities of importance, were the creations of the Company, and as such had no definite and specific rights on a reciprocal basis, though there is no doubt that their annexation was based on the principle 'of abandoning no just or honourable accession of territory.' The doctrine of lapse as applied by the Marquis of Dalhousie affected only the petty states. In fact, in the case of Indore, when Hari Rao Holkar died in 1843, after a period of miserable misgovernment which roused against him the fury of his own subjects, his mother was permitted to adopt a successor. Between 1826 and 1848 there were no less than fifteen cases of succession by adoption. In Indore, Datia, Orcha, Kotah, Udaipur, and twice in Dharangpur, the rulers were allowed to adopt, and in Dhar, Kishengarh, Karauli, Banswada and twice in Gwalior and twice in Indore the Ranis were allowed to adopt a successor.

But the right of adoption, which the Court of Directors in 1834 had instructed their Governor-General should be given only as an exception 'and should never be granted but as a special matter of favour and approbation,' was given after the Mutiny by special sanad to all Hindu rulers.

> Her Majesty being desirous that the government of the several princes and chiefs of India who now govern their own territories should be perpetuated and that the representation and dignity of their houses should be continued, I hereby in fulfilment of that desire convey to you the assurance, that on failure of natural heirs the adoption by yourself and the future rulers of your State of a successor according to Hindu Law and the custom of your race will be recognised and confirmed. Be assured that nothing shall disturb the engagement just

made to you as long as your house is loyal to the Crown, and faithful to the treaties, grants and engagements which record its obligations to British Government.

The new principles of loyalty and one-sided obligation imported into this will be discussed later. But this sanad closed a chapter which was full of bitterness and mistrust, and inaugurated a new era of relationship between the states and the Crown. There has been since then no case of an adoption being refused, or of the rights of adopted sons to succeed, in the case of failure of natural heirs, being questioned.

The claim of the Government of India to *regulate* succession in a sense going beyond its rights of recognition, which of course involve the right of veto on adequate grounds, has been denied by Indian states, and is hardly tenable at least in the case of the larger and sovereign rulers. In the case of natural heirs, the right of succession cannot be denied; though as sovereign power the British Government has the right of intervening where the natural heir is disqualified by madness or proved incapacity to rule. The only occasion of such intervention was the Manipur case. The Yuv Raj or heir apparent, who headed a disloyal conspiracy against the Maharajah, was proceeded against. On one occasion, too, the heir apparent of Cochin was publicly warned by the Resident [1] that if he persisted in certain objectionable courses of action his right of succession would be cancelled.

[1] C. Atchuta Menon, *Dewan Sankunni Menon*, p. 56.

The right of sanction claimed by the British Government over succession to the *gadi* has been contested by the princes as a body, and was raised at the earliest meetings of the Princes' Chamber. The princes there assembled questioned the prerogative that the Government of India had taken for itself beyond the terms of treaties, and held that the right of determining succession in case where any doubt existed must remain with the rulers; while in the case of well-defined succession from father to son, the present custom of the British Government sanctioning such succession should be given up. Discussion in the Princes' Chamber showed how strongly the Indian rulers felt on the point, and though no formal solution has been arrived at, the British Government appears to be anxious to find a formula more in consonance with the sovereignty and the treaty rights of the states.

In cases of disputed succession the right of the British Government to intervene and to decide is not denied. When the adoption has not been made in public or when the ruler died suddenly without making provision for the succession, the right of the paramount power to intervene cannot be questioned. The British Government has also the obligation to maintain the just rights of those whose claim to succeed the ruler desires unjustly to pass over. The case of Kashmir is in point. The Kashmir state was given to Maharajah Ghulab Singh and the 'heirs male of his body.' That is,

Speeches by Lord Chelmsford, vol. i. p. 476.

by the treaty which gave the sovereignty of Kashmir to the present house the right of succession, failing an heir by primogeniture, is vested in the nearest male descendant of Maharajah Ghulab Singh ; and Rajah Hari Singh was the person thus qualified. The desire of the late Maharajah was to see his adopted son the Prince of Poonch succeed to the *gadi* in supersession of the legal claim of Rajah Hari Singh, which is guaranteed in the treaty. The British Government had therefore every right to insist on the succession being in strict accordance with the dynastic law as settled by the treaty.

Nor can the right of the paramount power to ensure that the usages and customs governing succession shall be respected be denied. The succession law in Indian states is as varied as can be imagined. In Travancore and Cochin, succession is governed by matrilineal descent : the oldest living male member succeeds, the descent being counted through the female side.

Another right which the Government of India and its champions have claimed is that of nominating regencies and setting up minority administrations. Lord Mayo laid it down as a policy to set up regency administration whenever an opportunity arose and to use the occasion to push British claims, and to establish new rights and precedents. It was one of the tendencies of the new policy inaugurated by that Viceroy that even better than annexation is a regency under a British official. The right to

The Earl of Mayo, Hunter, Oxford, 1891, pp. 104-5.

constitute a regency was exercised by him not only when the ruler happened to be a minor. In the case of Alwar the Maharajah was practically deposed for maladministration, and a council of regency set up in 1870. In Gwalior a regency was set up in 1886, which, though under its own officials, was to carry on the administration with the sanction of the British Resident. The administration of Kotah in 1876 was carried on by a British political agent.

This right of nominating regents and setting up minority administrations has been claimed and exercised by the British Government as a part of its suzerainty. Whatever may be the obligations of the dependent principalities, such a claim is not accepted by the treaty states. The princes have steadily protested against such usurpation of sovereign rights. One of the main demands made in the Princes' Chamber was that the practice on this matter should be defined.

Wardship of the minor princes and control of their education have also been claimed on a feudalist interpretation of mutual obligations. Lord Curzon, speaking at the installation of the Maharajah of Alwar, declared that before entrusting a Maharajah with the administration of the state the British Government must satisfy itself 'that the young chief has received the education and the training . . . that will qualify him to rule over men.'

This certainly is a somewhat presumptuous claim. The lack of 'proper' education cannot take away hereditary right, and the implication of the Viceroy's speech, that if the British Government thinks that a young chief has not the requisite educational accomplishments, he may be prevented from succeeding to the *gadi*, is unwarranted. But since the time of Lord Mayo the British Government has interpreted liberally its obligations in respect of the education of young princes, realising that sojourn and training under special conditions in British territory tend to instil ideas of loyalty and allegiance into the future rulers.[1]

Besides the important right of determining succession and the various other rights that follow from it, the British Government has also claimed for itself the authority to depose, dispossess, degrade and punish Indian rulers. The main examples of deposition have been in Mysore, Baroda, Kashmir, Bharatpur and Alwar and Indore. Besides these, there have been forced abdications of political and constitutional importance in Indore, Nabha and Udaipur. The cases of deposition of rulers with sovereign rights have been those of Indore and Baroda. In Mysore the treaty which Wellesley made provided for the deposition of the Maharajah and the assumption of territory in certain definite eventualities. 'The Governor-General in Council shall be at liberty,' declared Article IV of the Treaty of Seringapatam, 'and shall haye full power and right either to introduce such regulations and ordinances as he shall deem expedient for the internal management and collection of revenues or

[1] See Maharajah of Gwalior's view as stated by Col. Luard, *Asiatic Review*, July, 1926.

for the better ordering of any other branch and department of the Government of Mysore ; *or to assume and bring under* direct management of the servants of the said Company *Bahadur* such part or parts of the territorial possessions of H.H. the Maharajah as shall appear to him the said Governor-General-in-Council necessary.' It is under this comprehensive clause that the Maharajah of Mysore was deposed in 1830, and the entire administration transferred into the hands of the British officers.

The case in Baroda was different. It is one of the earlier treaty states ; though the treaty of 1802 required the ruler to listen to advice given for the good of his country. The right of advice and friendly interference was expressly reserved, but the Gaekwar was, according to assurance of the Bombay Government, to remain unrestrained in internal affairs. The British Government had therefore a legal right to advise and interfere, and in the time of Malhar Rao Gaekwar, the Government of India on the ground of maladministration and court intrigue appointed a commission of enquiry, as a result of which the Gaekwar was 'warned.' Two years later a further charge was brought against the Maharajah, viz. of attempting to poison the British agent. The Gaekwar was arrested on the 13th January, and the proclamation which the Government issued declared that such an attempt would be a high crime against the Queen. He was tried before a special tribunal consisting of British officers and an Indian ruler and Sir Dinkar Rao ; and though the court was divided in opinion, the Government deposed him and his heirs were declared precluded from the succession.

The action against the Gaekwar was clearly high-handed and unlawful. Neither by treaty rights nor by recognised claims had the British Government the right of arresting and trying an Indian ruler. The arrest of the Gaekwar and his open trial [1] before a tribunal constituted flagrant breaches of agreement, and both the Indian people and the princes resented the proceedings strongly.[2] It was in fact with a view to placate the opinion of the princes that a new policy was inaugurated by the rendition of Mysore. It is significant that though graver cases have arisen, as in the instance of Nabha, neither arrest nor trial of any Indian prince has since taken place.

Veiled depositions in the form of forced abdications have been numerous. The Government has usually interfered in consequence of obvious maladministration, misuse of sovereign powers, or notorious crime. In the case of Indore in 1903 Maharajah Tukoji Rao Holkar was known to have been responsible for murder, and ruling rights were taken away from him. The case of Maharajah Ripudaman Singh of Nabha, which is the best known case of

[1] 1875.

[2] 'The true value of the Baroda case from the point of view of Indian political law lies in the number and importance of the political principles which it establishes, and in the fact that most or all of these principles received the expressed or implied concurrence of several leading chiefs. In the case of a state of the first consequence, and apart altogether from treaty rights, the Government of India . . . suspended and ultimately deposed an erring ruler.' C. L. Tupper, *The Indian Protectorate*, London, 1893, p. 118.

this kind, was even more complicated. Charges of three kinds were brought against the Maharajah. These were that he violated the sovereignty of the neighbouring state of Patiala by covert and overt acts of aggression, that he utilised the whole machinery of the state and the rights vested in him as ruler for purposes altogether criminal in intention and illegal in execution, and that he was associated with political movements outside his state which aimed at subverting the authority of the British Government. That these offences were of a nature to justify the most drastic action on the part of the paramount power is undeniable. But the most important feature of this case is the fact that the Maharajah was not deposed, but was given and exercised the option of abdicating. The political agent as well as the Government of India made it clear that it was only the 'odium of punishing a ruler' that prevented them from taking more drastic action, a significant enough commentary on the change that has come over the relations between the states and the Government of India since 1875, when a more powerful ruler was openly tried, deposed and exiled.

The resolution of the political department on the case of the Maharajah of Nabha sheds considerable light on the policy of veiled depositions.

> Of the charges set out in the eight annexures the findings have been against the Nabha Durbar on six. The Ishwar Kaur case (Annexure III) has fallen to the ground, and in the horse case (Annexure IV), the least important of all,

the Patiala Durbar have failed to establish that any offence was committed. In one case only (Annexure II) was there a violation of territorial rights, and though the acts of Nabha officials in that case call for censure, they are of little moment when compared with the revelations which have been made in Mr. Justice Stuart's report as a result of his enquiry into the six cases in which he has found against Nabha. Mr. Justice Stuart has in the main dealt with the cases individually, recording separate findings on each. It is left to the Government of India to synthetise the results and to draw its own inferences from the features which the cases possess in common.

The first of those features is that in all the cases in which the finding of the Special Commissioner is adverse to Nabha, the Nabha story is definitely false. In four of these cases (the cases against Abdul Aziz, Muhammad Yaqub and Abdul Latif, and the Nabha version of the Jiundan incident) the story has been deliberately fabricated by the Nabha police, and in the Pehdani case, it is clear that certain authorities in Nabha have supported a story which is false, though circumstances have prevented their putting the case into their own courts.

The second common feature is that all the fabrications and falsities have been aimed at one object, the injuring of Patiala. In the cases against Muhammad Yaqub and Abdul Aziz, Patiala officials were the victims. In the case against Abdul Latif, the victim was suspected of being a Patiala spy. In the Bugra case, an attempt has been made to implicate a Patiala sub-inspector, and in the Jiundan case, if the Nabha version had been believed, it would have meant that a number of Patiala police officers had been guilty of serious offences.

Thirdly, in all the cases in which the Nabha police have brought into court charges fabricated against persons connected with Patiala, the cases have been prosecuted to conviction in the Nabha courts on evidence which was utterly inadequate, and in circumstances which necessarily imply the complicity of judicial officers in the injustice which was perpetrated.

These three features show a deliberate perversion by highly-placed officials in the state of the whole machinery for the administration of justice for the purpose of damaging Patiala.

Ever since the Maharajah of Nabha succeeded his father, the Government of India have had abundant evidence that the whole policy of the state has been dominated by his personality, and it is inconceivable that the perversion of justice could have been reduced to a system of offence against Patiala, without the Maharajah's full general approval and active countenance. It is not, of course, to be expected that the Patiala Durbar would be able, or the Nabha Durbar willing, to produce specific proofs of this in every individual case. But it has been shown in Abdul Aziz's case that the Maharajah, in spite of having been given ample opportunity of seeing that the wrong was righted, allowed the proceedings to take their course, while in the case of Muhammad Yaqub, there is a definite finding that the false story in both its stages was false to the knowledge of the Diwan, and it is safe to assume in such matters that what was known to the Diwan was known to the Maharajah.

The Government of India must express the strongest condemnation of the state of affairs which the enquiry has revealed. In the written arguments presented to the Special Commissioner, stress is laid on the independence of the state in its internal affairs. The Durbar have apparently forgotten the Sanad of 1860 does not merely confer privileges, but that it also imposes obligations. Under Clause IV, the ruler of Nabha is bound to 'exert himself to every possible means in promoting the welfare of his people and the happiness of his subjects and redressing the grievances of the oppressed and injured in the proper way.' Clauses V and X bind him to loyalty and obedience to the British Crown and the British Government in India. All these obligations have been broken. The deliberate perversion of justice is a clear breach of Clause IV, the forcible infraction of Patiala's territorial rights is a breach of allegiance to the Crown, and the deliberate orientation of the policy of the Durbar towards the prosecution by force and fraud of the Durbar's own feud with its neighbour is a breach of the spirit of the well-known canon which prohibits hostilities between states.

The Government of India have been unable to trace any instance in the past in which they have been called on to pass orders on a case parallel to the present one, and they cannot conceive any more subtle or insidious form of oppression than the deliberate and methodical perpetration of injustice under cover of legal forms. It is not necessary to record here the measures which the Government of India would have been compelled to take in this case, because, while these measures were under consideration, the Maharajah of Nabha on his own initiative visited the agent to the Governor-General, Punjab States at Kasauli, and voluntarily expressed his desire to sever his connection with the administration of the state upon certain conditions. The Governor-General-in-Council has felt some hesitation in accepting this offer; but after a careful examination of the circumstances he has come to the conclusion that if certain necessary conditions are imposed, the offer may be accepted and that the advantages of a speedy settlement outweigh other considerations.

The anxiety of the Government of India to save themselves from the odium of deposing a ruler and their preference for a policy of veiled deposition comes out equally clearly in the Udaipur Maharana's case. The treaty with the Maharana of Udaipur does not belong to the earlier period. It is definitely on the basis of subordinate co-operation. Article III of Lord Hastings' treaty with Udaipur runs, 'The Maharana of Udaipur will always act in subordinate co-operation with the British Government and acknowledge its supremacy'; though a later clause lays it down that 'the Maharana shall always be absolute ruler of his own country.' The action against the present Maharana, however, taken as it was, with a suddenness which is difficult to understand, can hardly be brought under the comprehensive clause of subordinate co-operation. The facts are these. In 1921 there was much agrarian discontent in the state which led to something like an open outbreak. This was, however, put down by the Maharajah's forces. But taking advantage of this situation the Agent to the Governor-General wrote to the Maharajah demanding his abdication. The reasons given by Mr. Holland [now Sir Robert Holland] were that the Maharajah had become too old, and that he was attempting to concentrate too much in his own hands, and that as a result the administration had weakened. The Maharajah naturally resented this, and replied that he was perfectly ready to rectify any serious causes of complaint and to delegate some powers to his son.

This suggestion was accepted by the Government, which stated that it was fully aware of the Maharana's labours on behalf of his people throughout many years and of his concern for justice, and of His Highness having performed the duties of his high office with unselfish and unremitting zeal. But, added the Viceroy, 'the mere fact that the whole of the administrative arrangements have been concentrated in your Highness's hands has lately rendered your task impossible of achievement.'

The Udaipur case is valuable in two ways. It shows firstly that the Government is now fully aware of the odium that would attach to it if it were to take strong action against ruling princes, and secondly that in consequence thereof, a policy of meddling on minor pretexts has been developed. On the first point every state has now learnt to appeal to other rulers, and to interest them by pointing out that what affects one to-day may be used to-morrow as a precedent against another. The Maharana of Udaipur in his letter to the Government of India drew pointed attention to this. 'The importance of this to Indian states can scarcely be exaggerated. The more closely it is studied the more apparent does it become that the treatment of Udaipur is not only at variance with those expressions of policy contained in Chapter X of the Report on Indian Constitutional Reforms published in 1918. That report lays down the principle that in a composite society like India's, and in times when ideas are changing rapidly, the existence of states in which ideals of chivalry and personal devotion survive as the motive principle of the government has been more clearly seen to have an abiding value. There could be no more frank recognition of the wisdom of leaving Udaipur to be governed according to the traditions established for loyalty and devotion and the foolishness of attempting to force new ideas on those who do not desire them. These words were written at a time, to quote once again the Report, "when some rulers are perturbed by a feeling that the measure of sovereignty and independence granted to them by the British Government has not been accorded in full and they are apprehensive lest in process of time their individual rights and privileges may be swept away." There is a good ground now for that apprehension, for after the peremptory demand that His Highness should abdicate, no state can feel secure from intervention, even though there does not exist the one stipulated condition precedent to intervention.'

The second fact is that when in the anxiety 'to avoid the odium of public punishment of Rulers' the Government had to fall back on a policy of veiled deposition, its natural result was avoidable interference on trivial pretexts. The Udaipur case shows this, equally with other cases such as those of the Nawab of Palanpur, and the published correspondence between the Thakore Sahib of Rajkot and the political agent.

The only conditions which justify a deposition or

forced abdication are flagrant misuse of sovereign powers, open disloyalty involving breach of the alliance with the Crown, and breach of inter-state relations threatening the peace of the country. In any of these three circumstances, the paramount power would be entitled to interfere forcibly, but the instances that have been cited have demonstrated clearly that the Government of India has succeeded in extending the scope of intervention. An attempt has been made on the part of the Government of India to claim a close overlordship, which would, despite the clear provisions of the treaties, give it direct right of interference, with the threat of deposition in the background, on all and any matters. That this has been the tendency was frankly recognised in the Montagu-Chelmsford Report, and efforts have since been made through the Princes' Chamber and the conventions adopted by the Government to check its autocratic authority in this direction. Up to the present no change of policy has been adopted, especially as the princes are individually anxious that their cases should not come before committees and tribunals. In time, however, the machinery proposed by the Reforms of 1919 may be able to afford greater protection against the policy of deposition and forcible abdication which the Government of India held hanging over the heads of the rulers.

Other rights claimed and enforced by the British Government as appertaining to its sovereignty are those connected with the assumption and bestowal of titles, honours, salutes and precedence. So far as the rulers are concerned the Crown has claimed to be the fountain of all honour, and has tried as far as possible to restrict the assumption of new titles. No title is considered valid without the British Government's recognition, and any pompous addition which a prince may choose to assume is generally deprecated. The style and titles of most of the Indian princes date from a time anterior to their alliances with the British Government, and are mentioned in the treaty or in some other formal communication. A kharita from the Viceroy generally enumerates these titles in full and is a model of how a prince should be addressed. Thus, in a kharita to the Maharajah of Gwalior the following titles are enumerated :

> His Highness Muktar ul Mulk, Amir ul Iktedar Rufeeus shan wala Shikoh Mohta Shumi Dowran, Omdet ul Omrah, Maharajadhiraj Jayaji Rao Scindia Bahadur, Srinath mansoori Zaman Fidvee i Huzrat Malikeh Mooazma Rafeez Denjeh Inglistan, G.C.S.I., etc., etc.

Any further addition to this, if it is to be officially recognised, must be granted by the British Government, unless it could be proved that it was in use even before, though for the time in abeyance. Thus the Nizam was given the title of His Exalted Highness and was permitted to add to his dignities the designation of the Faithful Ally of the British Government. Hereditary titles are conferred and advanced on the princes as an exclusive right of the sovereign. The title of His Highness, again, is confined to those who enjoy more than eleven-gun salutes, though some of them enjoy no rights of sovereignty and possess no territory. Salutes are meant universally to indicate the status of the ruler, the highest class being entitled to twenty-one salutes. A table of salutes was drawn up in 1857 and published in 1864. It has been modified since then by additional grants and advancements. A distinction is made between dynastic and personal salutes. Thus, the Maharajah of Bikanir, who is entitled to a salute of seventeen guns, enjoys nineteen guns as a personal distinction. The Government also reserves for itself the right of decreasing or even taking away the salutes as a punishment. In 1866 the Maharajah of Datia was punished in this way by a reduction of his salute, which, on a later occasion, was wholly withdrawn. In 1870 the Maharajah of Jodhpur was also reduced in status in this manner. The cases in which salutes have been withdrawn or reduced are very rare, and the Government, anxious to 'avoid the odium of punishing a ruling prince,' has not of late resorted to this step, lest such action should arouse criticism throughout India and make an unfavourable impression on other ruling chiefs.

The limitation of titles and dignities is also enforced in other ways. The title of His or Her Highness, for instance, is confined to the ruler and his consort, and cannot be used officially outside the state by any other member of the ruling family, although inside the state these titles are often applied loosely. It is only by a specific grant that either the heir apparent or others closely connected with the ruler can claim that title. Thus, the Yuva Rajah of Mysore has been given the title of His Highness. Again the Government scrupulously avoids the use of the word prince as a title of sons of ruling princes. Thus, the son of a Maharajah, even if he is the heir apparent, is addressed as the Maharaj Kumar and that of a ruling nawab as Nawab Zada. The only princes officially recognised in India are the Prince of Arcot and Prince Akram Hussain Khan, the son of the last king of Oudh. There is, as is well known, no uniformity in the titles of heirs apparent, but the custom of the Government has been to recognise the local title. Thus, in the Sikh States, the heir apparent is called the Tikka Sahib and his consort the Tikka Rani. In Pudukkotta, he is styled Dorai Raja and Dorai Rani, while in most other Hindu states the title is Yuva Rajah and Yuva Rani. In Travancore and Cochin alone the title of Elaya Raja finds currency. The word royalty as a generic term is not recognised so far as Indian princes are concerned, and the families are alluded to not as royal families but as ruling families. Their Governments are styled Durbars, though the administrations of Hyderabad, Mysore and a few other states are permitted to use the higher term 'government.' In Hyderabad, however, the visitor can see in the centre of the city a building on which is written 'Government Post Office,' by which is meant not the post office of the Nizam but that of the British Government.

The grant of titles by the rulers is also limited. There was considerable hesitation on the part of the Government in recognising the titles granted by Indian rulers to British subjects, and it is only recently that the practice in this matter has been regulated. Now the rulers can give all Indian titles which the British Government itself does not give. The Nizam has of late been giving the title of maharajah, nawab and rajah even to British subjects, and though the Government has shown a hesitation in recognising them officially, it has not been so far able to prohibit their use or even to withhold semi-official recognition.

A clearer assertion of royal prerogative is the grant of Orders to the rulers themselves. The two Indian 'Orders' are the Most Eminent Order of the Indian Empire and the Most Exalted Order of the Star of India. The King is Patron and the Viceroy Grand Master of both. Each Order is divided into three sections: Companions, Knight Commanders and Knight Grand Commanders. Every ruler of any position is a member of one of these orders, while the first-class princes are invariably created Grand Commanders of one of the two and often of both. A smaller distinction than a G.C.I.E., for a ruler of first-class status, is an indication of serious displeasure, and the fact that the late Maharajah of Nabha, of all the ruling princes of India, was the only one without a title of this kind was, in fact, and was understood to be, a mark of almost open displeasure. Other

British titles like the Order of the Bath, Order of the British Empire, and the Victorian Order are given rarely. The late Mir Mahaboob Ali Khan was awarded a G.C.B. The present Maharajah of Bikanir is a K.C.B., and Raja Hari Singh of Kashmir is a K.C.V.O.

Rulers of India can accept foreign titles only with the permission of the British Government. That is implied in the clause which is invariably included in all treaties that the rulers in alliance with the British power should not have any connection with other states. Very few foreign distinctions are in fact held by Indians.

Precedence among the rulers is also decided, when a decision is necessary, as, for instance, at a Durbar, by the paramount power, whose decision is final and is enforced, as in the case of Jodhpur already quoted, with the severest penalties. An official order of precedence is laid down by the political department.

VI

EXTENSION OF IMPERIAL AUTHORITY

BESIDES the rights claimed on the basis of sovereignty examined in the previous chapter, the paramount power has claimed and assumed for itself, for military and other imperial considerations and international obligations, many rights which have affected the sovereignty of the princes. These are of a character more complicated in their legal and constitutional bearings and have to be studied with detailed care. The facts are scarcely in doubt. The authority of the paramount power has grown in many ways at the expense of the princes. Lord Chelmsford in the speech already quoted declared frankly that in the case of extra-territorial jurisdiction, railway and telegraph construction, limitation of armaments, coinage, currency and opium policy, and the administration of cantonments, the relations between the states and the Imperial Government have been changed. These changes have affected seriously the treaty position of Indian states, and must be taken into consideration in any attempt to understand the rights and authority of princes. They can be best studied under three heads: military, imperial and international.

From the military standpoint, the Government of India followed from the very beginning the policy which was enunciated as early as 1804 not only of defending the states from external aggression but of rendering them powerless against British power. 'The fundamental principle of His Excellency the Governor-General's policy in establishing subsidiary alliances is to place the states in such a degree of dependence on the British power as may deprive them of the means of prosecuting any measures hazardous to the security of the British Empire.'[1] So in its military policy so far as the states are concerned, the Government of India have consistently put this principle into operation by the establishment in the very heart of the states military cantonments with British jurisdiction from which it could quell an incipient rebellion or frustrate hostile movements. The cantonments at Secunderabad, Bangalore, Mhow and Ajmer demonstrate this. Secunderabad, though only a few miles from the capital of the Nizam, is a British area where the writ of His Exalted Highness does not run, and where British troops are quartered, so that the Subedar of the Deccan may feel at all times that Imperial power is near enough to him. The sovereignty of these areas has practically passed into the hands of the British Government, though in most cases they are acquired only on lease. They have been practically converted into asylums for

[1] Despatch of the Government of India to the Resident at Haiderabad, dated 4th February, 1804.

those who are disaffected with the rulers of the state and desire to further intrigues which would bring them within the law of the state. Thus, though Secunderabad is a mere speck within the area of the Nizam's territories, it is possible for those who are dissatisfied with the administration to gather together in that place and to carry on their political propaganda. For years a seditionist paper which reviled Travancore and its rulers was printed and published at Thangaserry, a small strip of British territory within the state. The complaint of the Maharajah of Udaipur in the letter quoted before was that agitators who had made Ajmer their base used to go and work among the ignorant peasants of his state. The rulers have no authority and their courts have no jurisdiction in these cantonments, which have become for them a visible sign of subjection.

An equally important encroachment for which greater justification could be made out is the cession of rights and jurisdiction over railway lines passing through the states. After the Mutiny the necessity of railways was realised and the High Command decided to build some main lines which would make transport of troops and material easy. The sanads granted in 1860 made clear provision for this. In the sanads given to Jind and Patiala, Lord Canning had expressly laid it down that 'the Raja will furnish at current rates through the agency of his own officers the necessary materials required for the construction of railways, railway stations, roads and bridges.' With the major states like Gwalior and Hyderabad, the question was settled by negotiations, but on the smaller tributary states the Government imposed the obligations as a part of military defence. In the Mysore agreement of 1881, which was drawn up after full experience and was more in the nature of a grant, it was laid down 'that the Maharajah should grant such land as may be required for the construction of railways and transfer full jurisdiction within such lands.'

The question of jurisdiction on the railways, which manifestly makes an inroad on the judicial independence of Indian states, will be dealt with in another chapter. It is of importance here to note that railway lines intersect most states now and on these lines the rulers of Indian states have but insignificant rights. The only state that has so far refused to come into line upon railway policy is Kashmir. The basis of all railroad claims on Indian states is the principle that communication, transport, and mail service are parts of the rights of military defence for which the exclusive authority rests with the British Government. The subsidiary treaty is fundamentally a treaty which guarantees military protection, and undertakes on the part of the Central Government the duty of defending the states and the rulers. This right which the states have surrendered to the British involves the right to take all military measures, and as in modern warfare railway transport, mail service and the maintenance of unbroken line of communications are most essential, the rights of the paramount power in this connection cannot be disputed.

Without the permission of the Government of India, the states cannot build railways unless they are absolutely unconnected with other lines and are purely for internal purposes. The only lines so far undertaken on this basis are the Mysore-Aruvikkara line undertaken by the Mysore State, and the Sipri line undertaken by the Maharajah of Gwalior.

Telegraph lines, telephone system and postal arrangements are also included in the defensive scheme. Telegraphs are worked as Government departments, and have been established all over India, including the states. Officers employed by the Government of India with their staffs reside in the states, inspect local offices and exercise jurisdiction. The states in which these telegraph offices exist and through which the lines pass have no authority, and, though allowed certain privileges in their use, are treated as having no special right. No one thing has so emphasised the extension of the authority of the Central Government as the telegraph offices, which are exclusively manned, controlled, supervised, even when the offices are located in Indian states, by the officers of the Government of India. The same is true of the trunk telephones.

The postal system may also be considered in this connection. Most of the important states like Hyderabad have their own internal postal system. But the British Government for purposes of all-

Indian communication has introduced into most of the states the British postal system, with its own offices, officials and superintending staff. In Gwalior by special arrangement an exchange postal system is working. Generally speaking, the British post offices, even when established in state territory possessing its own postal arrangement, are managed by British officials. This duplication of services embodies an assertion of the authority of the paramount power, for otherwise by agreement between the departments an easy system of exchange should have been possible.

In all these three matters, railways, telegraphs and postal service, policy tends unavoidably towards the extension of the sovereign rights of the paramount power. They provide the chains by a judicious utilisation of which the states may slowly be bound hand and foot, as a matter of natural evolution, before they could awake to the reality of their position. It cannot be denied that these extensions of rights, though they are counter to the sovereignty of the states and amount in some cases to an encroachment, have been made in the interests of Indian unification, especially in the matter of defence. Their influence in stimulating the growth of a feeling of Indian nationality cannot be denied. But they have helped to transform the independent states of India into constituent members of an Indian polity with limited powers dependent on the will of the Central Government. It is for this reason that, though much pressure was put on them, both Afghanistan and Nepal refused the extension of British postal and telegraphic services, fearing lest these appurtenances of civilisation should affect their status as independent states.

A further phase of Imperial expansion dictated by military and defensive considerations has been the definite limitation of state forces. The earlier treaties contain in general no clause which sets a specific limit to the military forces to be maintained by the rulers, but as the main purpose of those agreements is to entrust the defence of the state to the paramount power and to maintain a subsidiary force for that purpose, the question of limiting the state forces is clearly within the competence of the Central Government. In fact, one of the main articles of the treaty with the Nizam (1st September, 1798) was for the purpose of disbanding the French regiment in Hyderabad service. Most of Wellesley's trouble with Oudh was on the score of the Vizier's ill-disciplined forces, the reduction of which the Governor-General demanded in the interests of peace and security. Writing to the Secret Committee of the Court of Directors, Wellesley declared that he was intending to put into execution such a reform of the Nabob Vizier's military establishments as should eliminate all future danger from the frontier of Oudh, and that he had requested the Vizier 'to disband under certain regulations a proportional part of his own useless and dangerous force.' 'The conduct of different corps of Your Excellency's troops,' wrote the Governor-General to the Nawab, 'had in several instances previously to the approach of Zeman Shah abundantly manifested that no reliance could be placed either in their fidelity or in their discipline. Many of them had mutinied and were prevented from proceeding to acts of open violence against Your Excellency's person by the presence of the Company's troops'; and on this ground immediate disbandment of a large portion of it was demanded.[1] The rebellion in Travancore was also due to this cause. The Company demanded that the Carnatic battalion should be disbanded. As Cochin had been brought under the Company's protection and Mysore had ceased to menace the frontier of Travancore, there was no necessity for the state to keep up such a large force; but as it was not in the treaty, the demand was resisted and the Dewan led a revolt, which was crushed. The chief Northern Indian states were allowed to maintain large military establishments of their own in the early days. The Maharajah Scindia in special maintained a large and unwieldy establishment for a considerable time. This was the cause of much internal trouble in the state. In the intrigues that followed Doulat Rao Scindia's death in 1827, the army took sides and a civil war ensued. The army of Scindia became a real menace to the state, and its violence led to British intervention in 1843, when Lord Ellenborough ordered General Gough to march on Gwalior and demand the disbandment of the army.

[1] *Wellesley's Despatches*, 189, 193.

During the time of the Mutiny the danger of these forces was again manifested. Holkar's troops rose in revolt and Scindia's forces left their maharajah and joined Tantia Topi and the heroic Queen of Jhansi. In no Hindu or Muslim state was the loyalty of the troops above suspicion during the days of the Mutiny; and even in Hyderabad it was only the firm hand of Salar Jung that kept the military under control. After the Mutiny there was naturally much distrust, and the Government of India was inclined to consider the troops of the Indian states as a source of danger to its safety. But a better policy was soon discovered in which the safety of India as a whole and the dignity and sovereignty of Indian states were combined for mutual benefit. It was Lord Dufferin who first saw the possibility of developing the military resources of the states for the benefit of the Empire while at the same time affording an opportunity for the military spirit in the states to survive. The force was to be entirely under Indian control, and naturally there was much difference in the discipline as well as efficiency of the units. They were, however, used for some field service on the frontier before Lord Curzon's time, and because of the experience so gained that Viceroy recognised the necessity for co-ordinating the command of the forces maintained by the states.

The present position of the Indian state forces as an effective second line defence has been well recognised by the authorities. Lord Curzon was the first to utilise them for service outside India, and since then they have won great distinction in the Great War on many fronts and in the Afghan war. The Bikaner camel corps, the Gwalior, Patiala and Mysore forces were of great service, and their efficiency and their courage were recognised by the British high command. These forces, though nominally loaned at the discretion of the princes, may be said to be maintained for the service of the Central Government. They are trained and equipped with the help of British Officers, who are called military advisers. There is a permanent staff whose chief officer is called military adviser-in-chief.[1] After the war these troops have been increased in strength and reorganised in the categories, class A, class B and class C. Class A consists of troops reorganised on the basis of the post-war experience and armed and equipped in accordance with the Indian army system. They are kept in the highest state of efficiency, fit for field service. Class B is equipped and maintained on the pre-war basis, and class C is a militia not permanently embodied. The total number of troops of all arms in state service amounts to 27,030.

These are not all the military obligations of the states. The later treaties expressly lay down the obligation of the states to furnish troops according to their means at the requisition of the Government, which amounts to a right on the part of the para-

[1] See *Army in India and its Evolution*, p. 157, Supdt. Govt. Printing, Calcutta, 1924.

mount power to claim the whole resources of the states in case of war. But so far as the states in earlier alliance are concerned this is not the fact. There the military obligation is entirely on the side of the British Government, but with the change of time the position has also changed, giving the paramount power greater claims and more extensive rights in case of war, as the obligation of defence is inherent in the clause that the enemies of either are the enemies of both. There is, however, no justification, legal or constitutional, for the statement of Lee Warner that in times of war there is 'unlimited responsibility'[1] for the princes. In the case of the earlier states, it was in order to relieve them of military responsibility and of the Company's defence being made to depend upon their irregular and inefficient troops that they were forced to subsidise British troops, and to pay for it in cash or by the assignment of land. When their responsibilities have thus been taken over expressly and consideration received year by year or, as in the case of the Nizam and Scindia, territories annexed instead, the claim to make 'unlimited demands in case of war' cannot be maintained from any point of view except that of force. Lee Warner's argument to prove that the paramount power possesses any right that it cares to claim is based on analogies and *a priori* considerations which can scarcely invalidate historic facts.

The political and legal encroachments on the

[1] Lee Warner, pp. 234-5

rights of Indian states have been equally fundamental. In coinage and currency, in customs and fiscal policy, in claiming direct allegiance from the subjects of Indian states, in the arrangements of extradition, the paramount power has assumed legal and constitutional rights which have made serious inroads upon the guaranteed prerogatives of the major Indian sovereignties.

Coinage with rights of separate currency has been one of the rights of sovereignty from time immemorial in India. During the time of the Moghuls, the emperors took special care that their subordinate princes should not issue their own coins. With the breakdown of the Moghul power each state set up its own mint and coined currency of its own. Thus, when the Company made alliances with Indian states the right of having their own coins was enjoyed by most states. This was found by the British Government later on to be an inconvenience, and for a long time it has been the policy of the Government to impose, without obvious violation of rights, its own currency on the states. It was laid down that when the coinage rights of a state had fallen into abeyance they could not be revived, and that coins which had for some time ceased to be current should not be re-introduced. In the Instrument of Rendition by which Mysore was handed back, it was specifically laid down that 'the separate coinage of Mysore State which has long been discontinued should not be revived.' The state of Jinjira was prevented from reviving its coin. In most of the states British coins are now in general use, and have become in some cases the exclusive currency. In Hyderabad there is, however, the Sicca rupee, and the Government of His Exalted Highness the Nizam issued currency notes immediately after the war, thus extending the rights of coinage without either previously informing or waiting for the approval of the Government of India. This fact is of importance, as the policy of the Government has been to oppose the extension of privileges and prerogatives in this direction. Faced with a *fait accompli* it was powerless to intervene. The principle which is involved here is of value. Udaipur, it will be remembered, has separate coinage, and one of the complaints against the Maharana was that the exchange between British India and the Udaipur State was complicated. Travancore has on paper a rupee which, however, is not coined though all state accounts are kept in it, and half-rupee and quarter-rupee silver coins are issued. In Rajputana there are in circulation twelve different gold mohurs, some of which are issued annually, and each state has a different rupee which differs slightly in value from the coins of the same name. There is, practically speaking, no system for recalling an older issue and replacing it by new coinage. In Alwar (1905) and in Bikaner (1903) British coins were introduced during a minority under orders from the political agent acting as President of Council.[1]

[1] *Currencies of Hindu States of Rajputana*, W. W. Webb, London, 1893, Introduction.

The British Government on various pleas have at different times tried to make rules about the minting of coins and about their use. It is laid down that mints should be worked only in the capital, and only so much should be coined as is absolutely necessary for currency in the states. In a few minor states pressure has been brought to bear for the free circulation of even the smaller British coins. The objection from the states' point of view is twofold: first, that this is an invasion on the guaranteed sovereign rights of the state, and, second, that it is an interference with a source of legitimate revenue. Besides these two points, there is also the consideration that in some states at least the smallest unit of general currency is even smaller than the pie, which is a matter of great importance for the poorer classes.

But in spite of all this, the universalisation of the British rupee and its fractions has been one of the main and obvious symbols of the extension of British rule. Everywhere in India the rupee is legal tender, with the result that even as in Hyderabad where there is an absolutely different currency, the British coins circulate freely and create a delicate and complicated exchange problem. The states are also deprived of their just and legitimate profits from coinage, and with the increasing hold of the British rupee and the nickel anna, their monetary rights are in danger of being whittled away. In this the Central Government has also been helped by the presidency banks, which have had a practical monopoly of banking business in the states also. Since these deal only in British currency their activities have gone a great way in making the British paper issue as well as the smaller British coins current in the states. In these as well as other matters, the European banks have greatly helped Government tendencies.

The extension of British authority so far as customs are concerned has been mainly in relation to sea-borne trade. As only Travancore, Baroda and Cutch of the larger Indian states have sea coasts, no general policy has been necessary. With Travancore, the British Government has entered into an inter-portal convention by which the state is compensated for its loss of sea customs by a consolidated sum. So far as land customs and transit duties are concerned, the states have so far maintained their rights, though the Government has been anxious to secure a unified policy on this matter. A Zollverein on the German model has been the British ideal, but the states have resisted it, to a large extent successfully. Their complaint has been that the protective customs which the Government of India are now introducing amount to an indirect taxation on the Indian states, and thereby involve a breach in their sovereign rights. The princes have put forward a claim to share the customs receipts, since their subjects also contribute to it. Speaking at the Dusserah Session of Mysore Representative Assembly (1924) the Dewan of Mysore declared that it was unjust that the Government of India should impose indirect taxation on the states, and claimed that a method should be devised by which the states could be given their due share. It is also known that a committee of the Princes' Chamber examined this question and the matter is now being discussed between the states and the Government.

The most important matter in which the political authority of the Government of India has extended is the claim put forward about the direct allegiance of the subjects of Indian states to the British sovereign. It was in the case of the Manipur rebellion that the British Government enunciated the principle that the subjects of Indian states owed direct allegiance and loyalty to the British throne. In previous revolts this question was never directly brought under discussion. In the Travancore rebellion the view was taken that the revolt was against the Maharajah and that British intervention was only for the purpose of upholding the rajah's authority. In the case of Coorg war was actually declared on the rajah, and his subjects were assumed to be enemies and not rebels. The actual *casus belli* was provided by the action of the rajah in imprisoning the British envoy. No claim was made that as the rajah was a subordinate ally his subjects bore allegiance to the Company. This farther assertion of sovereign rights was reserved for a much later occasion. The opportunity was provided by the Manipur State. The brother of the ruling rajah rose in rebellion and installed the Jubraj on the *gadi*.

The British Government recognised the Jubraj, but demanded that the brother who had raised the standard of revolt should be expelled. This the Jubraj refused to do, and a British force entered the territory, deposed the Jubraj, and tried him. He was sentenced to be hanged. The subjects of the Manipur State were enjoined by proclamation to take warning by the punishment inflicted. This was an attempt to claim direct allegiance from the subjects of Indian states. The question whether in an act of resistance by a ruler, the subjects of the state should loyally obey the Maharajah cannot be answered completely by a proclamation from the Government of India. Subjects of a state like that of the Nizam owe their immediate duty and allegiance to their sovereign. The claim put forward that the Imperial authorities can dissolve this allegiance by proclamation is tenable rather on the basis of superior strength or political expediency than of law or of treaty obligations. The idea that new obligations can be created or established rights taken away in the case of states in alliance by the Government of India issuing either a circular letter or a proclamation is not sound. But such action, though it could establish no legal claim, is a clear enough indication of the tendency towards imperial authority. The Government of India has exerted itself to push forward new claims and to extend old ones. For this purpose, constitutional, legal and feudal theories have been brought into use. Each in its turn has served to deprive the rulers of some part of their authority, or to give to the Central Government some new basis for intervention.

The subsidiary treaties uniformly contain a clause restricting the external sovereignty of the states which enter the alliance. They are constrained by agreements not to enter into negotiations with foreign powers. They cannot receive diplomatic or consular representatives from other powers, and even the employment of non-British Europeans without the express sanction of the Government of India is strictly prohibited. Their subjects in other countries are classed as British citizens, and Europeans in Indian states are under the guarantee and protection of the paramount power. It is clear that so far as external relations are concerned the authority of the Central Government is absolute and open to no kind of objection.

The treaties with the states are explicit on this point of relationship with non-Indian powers. The purpose of the treaties, as was pointed out in an earlier chapter, was the fear of foreign intervention, and even in the earlier treaties the stipulation is made that foreigners should not be employed or negotiations with foreign states undertaken without the sanction of the Government of India. Parliament itself declared in 1876 that ' the several princes and states in India in alliance with Her Majesty have no connections, engagements or communication with foreign powers and the subjects of such princes and states are when residing or being in places hereinafter referred to entitled to the protection of the British and receive such protection equally with the subjects of Her Majesty.' This principle has been accepted, and the natural implications of it, such as the responsibility of the Government to afford protection to Indian state subjects abroad and to safeguard their interests, have also been recognised.

The international obligation of the British Government so far as Indian states are concerned involve certain definite rights which have inevitably restricted the sovereignty of the states. The Government is bound to protect the lives and property of foreigners and to afford them the enjoyment of just rights and privileges. This means a direct control in the internal administration of the state and a right of intervention. There is a farther obligation on the part of the sovereign power to see that international agreements entered into with foreign powers are honoured in the states. For example, treaties entered into with certain European states give the nationals of those states the right of being tried before a jury of their own countrymen, and as in foreign relations the British Government represents Indian states also, the obligation so undertaken is binding on the rulers of the states, and the supreme Government has the right as well as the duty of enforcing it even within the jurisdiction of the protected rulers. In such questions as the extradition of criminals, or rules with regard to navigation, or imperial enactments validating international agreements on such questions as the opium traffic or the white slave traffic, the authority of the Central

Government is unquestionably implied in the restriction of the external sovereignty of the states. Since the states have no separate international status, their maritime boundaries in the case of Travancore, Cochin, Baroda and other states having a coast-line, and the land frontiers in the case of Kashmir, can only be regarded as British boundaries, and admiralty and maritime rights, in the former case, are vested in the paramount power.

The obligations of the Imperial Government to foreign powers both in war and in peace are, of course, binding on the states. Thus the exportation of contraband material in time of war, when the empire is neutral, to countries engaged in hostilities, and other acts of that nature which the paramount power has undertaken to prohibit within its own territories, cannot be allowed within the states. In the same manner the obligation to surrender criminals, if undertaken by the paramount power in treaties with other states, is binding on the rulers.

The obligation of the British Government with regard to the subjects of Indian states in international matters is also well defined. Passports for all foreign travel are issued by the Government of India, and no difference is made between the subjects of His Majesty and those who own immediate allegiance to their own rulers. The preamble of the statute 39 and 40 Victoria, Cap. 46, quoted before, expressly states that the subjects of Indian rulers are entitled to the protection of the British and receive such protection equally with the subjects of His Majesty.

In the agreement with the Sultan of Maskat it was expressly stipulated that 'subjects of the native states of India who may commit offences within the Maskat dominions shall be amenable to the political agent and the consul's court in the same way as British subjects.'

Besides this legitimate expansion of authority in matters relating to external sovereignty, the Government of India has also claimed and enforced its right to prohibit inter-statal negotiations. The treaties made with the rulers recognise no uniform principle on this question. In the treaty made by Wellesley with Alwar State, it was laid down that 'if any misunderstanding should arise between the Maha Rao Rajah of Alwar and the Sarkar of any other chieftain, Maha Rao Rajah will in the first instance submit the cause of dispute to the Company's Government that the Government may endeavour to settle it amicably. If from the obstinacy of the opposite party no amicable terms can be settled then Maha Rao Rajah may demand aid from the Company's government.' It will be remembered that in the original treaty with the Dowlat Rao Scindia, the British Government undertook not to enter into negotiations with Rajput states, and left that prince in unfettered external independence except so far as negotiations with principal states and powers were concerned.

But in most cases the paramount power has expressly provided against direct negotiations between states. The treaty with the Nizam stipulated 'that in the event of any differences arising, whatever adjustment of them the Company's Government, weighing all matters in the scale of truth and justice, may determine shall meet with full approbation and acquiescence.' Clauses of a similar character are inserted in most treaties, while in the treaty negotiated by Lord Hastings with the Maharana of Udaipur, it is declared that all disputes should be submitted to the arbitration and award of the British Government. Often enough there have been occasions in which relations between neighbouring states like Kutch and Morvi, Patiala and Nabha, Travancore and Cochin, have been strained to the point of hostilities, and the action and authority of the Central Government alone have prevented bloodshed. The dispute about the Kutal Manikkiyam Devasthanam in Cochin State territory reached such a point that the then Maharajah of Travancore wrote that but for the British Government his troops would have marched on Cochin by that time. The violation of Patiala sovereignty by Nabha was one of the charges against Maharajah Ripudaman Singh, and it was amply proved that there was an attempt on the part of the Nabha State to encroach on the territorial sovereignty of its neighbour. Between Kutch and Morvi disputes came to such a head that the Central Government was forced to intervene. The rulers have no right of private war, and by the surrender of their external authority they have abandoned the claim to enforce their demands by appeal to arms. The states have admittedly entered into an alliance of subordination. Wherever the rights they enjoy would lead to a conflict with the rights expressly abandoned by them, it is clear that they should abide by the decision of the Central Government. Inter-statal disputes, therefore, must be settled by the award of the paramount power, and no state has the right of refusing to abide by the decision of the Government.

This surrender of external authority naturally extends the claims of the central power in relation to the administration of justice with regard to European, British and foreign nationals, and the establishment of extra territorial authority within the states. Just as the subjects of Indian rulers are under the protection of the British Government when in foreign countries, the subjects of other independent powers are diplomatically under the protection of Britain when in Indian states, and the British Government is answerable for their safety and security while sojourning in and travelling through those states. This has been expressly recognised by the rulers. The Nizam in a notification announced that in the event of any discussion or dispute arising among Europeans, the Resident at Hyderabad or any other officer whom he may consider it desirable to vest with the same authority, shall be empowered to enquire into and punish any such offences. This acceptance of outside jurisdiction in the case of foreigners is a corollary to the surrender of external sovereignty. So far as foreign powers are concerned, Indian states have no recognised status and have completely lost their identity in the British Empire. The mere delegation of external authority would not, however, mark the disappearance of international sovereignty when the right was never expressly abandoned as in the case of Nepal and Afghanistan in recent times. The right of Nepal was never questioned, and that of Afghanistan was denied only indirectly by an agreement between Russia and England to which Amir was not a party. This, however, is not the case with Indian states, each of which has surrendered its rights and merged internationally in the British Empire. In 1853 the ruler of Bhopal was informed that only the political agent had jurisdiction over European British subjects. The same happened in Travancore, where, in spite of recognised precedent, the British Government insisted that only European magistrates should try Europeans, though no less an authority than Sir Henry Maine held that legally Travancore had every right to try Europeans, and no proclamation of Parliament can take away its jurisdiction,[1] and a compromise was reached by the Maharajah agreeing to appoint a European magistrate specially for the purpose.

Extra territorial jurisdiction in Indian states is a very complicated subject, especially as its forms are numerous and widely different. Besides jurisdiction over British and foreign subjects, which is of a capitulatory character, there are a number of

[1] *Memoir of Sir Henry Maine, with Select Speeches and Minutes*, Minute dated April 19, 1869, p. 400.

other matters in which the Government of India, in virtue of its executive authority, exercises jurisdiction. The capitulatory provisions about European (including American) nationals extended over most countries in Asia, and was abolished only recently in Turkey. In China, Siam, Persia and Egypt, they are still in force. Of the other forms of jurisdiction the most important are those relating to the right of appeal in non-sovereign states, jurisdiction in cantonments and residencies, and the special authority exercised in railway tracts. In many of the non-sovereign states which may strictly be called feudatories, the British Government has the right of appeal in the case of capital punishments. There are also other states in which the Resident has to be informed, though his formal sanction is not required, before capital punishments are carried out. Besides these cases of rights expressly reserved, a whole system of British jurisdiction not based on the legislative sanction of British India but on the executive authority of the Governor-General in Council has developed in Kathiawad, Mahikanta and other places where the conflicting jurisdictions of petty chiefs make judicial administration otherwise impossible. Superior political courts of justice and a sort of federal court presided over by an officer of the British Government exercise appellate jurisdiction in Kathiawad.[1] A similar kind of agency court, or 'international tribunal' in a restricted sense of the term, exists also in Rajputana. The

[1] See note on Kathiawad, Appendix I, Note I.

rivalry of Rajput rulers and the absence of modernised codes of law and judicial institutions in most states made such an institution necessary. But circumstances in Rajputana differ materially, so far as the powers and rights of rulers are concerned, from those in Kathiawad. The common court had to be organised without obvious infringement of the sovereignty of the states. The method devised was a court of ' Vakils ' or ambassadors, consisting of the representatives of the chief states in attendance on the agent to the Governor-General, and this body was to form the Court of Appeal. The jurisdiction is confined to securing justice for subjects outside the territory of their own chiefs. In states where the right of capital punishment can be exercised only with the permission of the Resident, or where administration of criminal justice has to be supervised by him, the extra territorial jurisdiction of the Government of India is implied as a fundamental part of the native state constitution.

More extensive and altogether on a different footing is the jurisdiction exercised by the British Government in cantonments and stations occupied by the military. In those areas the state Governments exercise no sovereign functions and British authority is exercised under the executive authority of the Government of India. Towns like Secunderabad and Bangalore cantonment are more or less in the position of Shanghai, Canton and other ' concessions ' in China, with this difference, however, that the authority exercised in the treaty ports is international. The cantonment towns, though generally leased to Government, are completely under British jurisdiction, but the reversionary right of possession in case the garrison is withdrawn remains with the state. Thus, when the force stationed in Quilon was withdrawn, British jurisdiction in the cantonment ceased therewith, and the Gwalior fort was handed back, in 1885, to Maharajah Scindia. Analogous to this, but recognised everywhere in international law as an ambassadorial right, is the right of jurisdiction within the residency and the grounds attached to it. The residence is inviolable, and the British Government has invariably treated an attack on the residency as rebellion.

In the tracts acquired for the purposes of railway construction also the right of external jurisdiction is recognised by Indian states. But the 'full jurisdiction' granted on these tracts is only for purposes strictly connected with railway administration. This was decided by the Privy Council in the case of Mahommed Yusuf Uddin *v.* the Queen Empress (7th July, 1897). The case arose from the arrest on the warrant of a Simla magistrate of a person in the precincts of a railway tract assigned to the British Government in 'full jurisdiction.' The Privy Council held that full jurisdiction meant in this connection only jurisdiction for the purpose of railway administration, and that for other purposes the territory should be considered as being under the sovereignty of the Nizam. For purposes of convenience and efficiency it is no doubt necessary that jurisdiction in the railways should be uniform. But when Indian states build railways unconnected with main trunk lines under Government, as Mysore is doing, the question of separate jurisdiction vanishes.

The Governor-General in Council has, of course, no right to legislate for the subjects of Indian states residing in state territory. But even in state territory the Indian Legislative Council has jurisdiction over the servants and subjects of the Company. The Government of India Act of 1833 (Section 43) laid down that the Council was empowered to legislate for all servants of the said Company within the dominions of the princes and states in alliance with the said Company. In 1865 this power was further extended to subjects of the Company as well as its servants. It was declared expedient to enlarge the powers of the Governor-General in Council by authorising him to make laws and regulations for all British subjects within the dominions of Indian princes. Even so far as the subjects of Indian princes are concerned, some legislative power has been assumed by the Government. The Slave Trade Act of 1876 (39 and 40 Vict. Cap. 46) enacted that the subjects of Indian princes committing certain offences on the high seas should be punished as if the offence was committed on British territory. This is evidently based on the principle that so far as international law is concerned, the subjects of Indian princes outside their own territory are to be considered to have the duties, obligations and rights of British-born subjects.

In all these matters there has been a clear and undeniable restriction of the rights of Indian states. But since each of these relates either to military or to international affairs, a justification could be found for them in the surrender of diplomatic rights which is the one invariable characteristic of all subsidiary treaties. External sovereignty implies the right to accredit and receive ambassadors, to ally or negotiate with any power for specific purposes, and to pursue common ends between a number of states for purposes of trade, defence, etc. As the Indian states have surrendered all these, the extension of British authority in purely external matters cannot be objected to, and is based on unquestionable treaty rights. But the same could not be said of internal intervention, which has also been so extended as to give the central authority almost unlimited rights.

VII

INTERVENTION IN INTERNAL AFFAIRS

INTERVENTION in the internal affairs of the states has been the fertile ground of controversy and ill-feeling between the Indian states and the Government of India. In the treaties with the sovereign states in India (in this connection the differentiation already made and historically insisted upon from the time of Wellesley to the Princes' Chamber must be kept in mind) there is invariably a clause that the ruler who is entering into alliance with the Company is left ' absolute ' in the internal affairs of his country. The treaty with the Maharajah of Gwalior stipulates that no officer of the Honourable Company should ever interfere in the internal affairs of the Maharajah's Government. The same pledge occurs in the treaty with Holkar, and appears in slightly modified forms in all important treaties. Even in the treaty with the Maharana of Udaipur, which is really one of subordinate co-operation and not of reciprocal alliance, it is expressly declared that ' The Maharana shall always be absolute ruler of his own country.' The restriction thus imposed on British intervention in the internal affairs of Indian states is most explicit, and has been accepted as binding on the British sovereign in the proclamation of the Queen. Yet there is nothing more certain than that the Government of India has tended from the earliest days to enlarge its interventions and to reduce the authority of the rulers. Wellesley bore witness to the fact as early as 1806 when he declared that, though the treaties stipulated that the rulers should be independent in all the operations of its internal management, the door was necessarily opened to the interference of the British Government in every concern.[1] The Company intervened in the affairs of Indian states for its own profit, as the history of the relations with Oudh traced in an earlier chapter conclusively shows. Even in states with which the treaty relations were on a footing almost of equality, as with Gwalior before 1843, the policy of the Company was to intervene either to force an annexation or to replenish its empty coffers. In the early days of Junkoji Scindia an attempt was made to get him to abdicate and to assign the territory to the British Government, and Mr. Cavendish, the Resident, who refused to be a party to this nefarious plot, was accused of having 'allowed a favourable chance to escape of connecting the Agra to the Bombay Presidency.'[2]

Intervention in fact was the settled policy, and was announced as such. Even among nations of equal status and recognised international independence there exists undeniably the right of remon-

[1] *Op. cit.*

[2] John Hope, *House of Scindia*, p. 28.

strance which, when exercised by a stronger power or under circumstances of a difficult character, becomes almost an irresistible interference. Thus, it is well known that the European powers publicly remonstrated against the policy of Austria in Italy, which really amounted to internal interference in the affairs of a first-class power. In recent times the action of the King of Belgium in the Congo provided matter for intervention by other powers.

But the interference of the Government of India in the internal affairs of Indian states is not of this nature. It is comprehensive and pervading, it reduces to a shadow the authority of the ruler, and it assumes under the cover of indigenous agency full sovereign rights, though obviously this is directly contrary to treaty engagements. Sir George Campbell, an eminent authority, writing in 1852 declared, 'it must be admitted that in our interference with the internal concerns of the native states we do in practice go much beyond the letter of original stipulations. . . . Whatever the original stipulation, there is in fact almost no state with the internal affairs of which we have not had something to do. There is no uniform system, and it is almost impossible to give any *definite explanation of what things we do meddle with and what we do not*.'[1] In a minute of 1860, Lord Canning stated, 'The Government of India is not precluded from stepping in to set right such serious abuses in a native government as may threaten any part of the country with

[1] Sir George Campbell, *Modern India*, London, 1852.

anarchy or disturbance nor from assuming temporary charge of a native state when there shall be sufficient reason to do so. *Of this necessity the Governor-General in Council is the sole judge* subject to the control of Parliament.' This, adds his Lordship, 'has long been our practice.' Lord Northbrook, writing to the Gaekwar in 1875, claimed the right of intervention in case of misrule, of which the Governor-General in Council is, of course, the sole judge. In fact, it is a known and notorious fact that until recently the intervention of the Resident extended to all conceivable spheres of administration.

To base the right of intervention on the minutes of the Governor-General, the memorandum of the political department or upon expressions of opinion by legal authorities in the pay of the Government of India, is to forget that there are two parties in the case whose relation to one another is expressly defined by treaty. Expressions of opinion of the nature of Lord Canning's minute or the circular letter of the Government of India in the Manipur case, or Lord Hardinge's note to Kashmir in 1848, can therefore have no importance except as showing the mind of the British Government. Ample evidence of this kind is to be found in official documents that the British Government has all along desired to extend its authority in the internal affairs of Indian states. During the weak reign of some ruler or through the agency of a minister nominated by the Resident, the Government interferes in one matter after another, and this broadens from precedent to precedent until the sovereignty of the ruler virtually disappears. Thus, in Travancore, all appointments carrying a salary of above 500 rupees have at present to be notified to the Resident, though this is a claim which has only been put forward comparatively recently.[1] It is known that in other equally important states the authority of the Resident has grown only by the accumulation of precedents, most of them adventitious and many of them forced on the ruler in times of weakness.

Intervention is not always in the form of formal correspondence or authoritative insistence. The advice of the Resident is usually an order or a command, and, as there is no limitation of sphere in the matters of advice, it is clear that except in cases where Residents feel it their duty to leave Indian rulers to a large extent to themselves (and such cases are few) their authority is all-comprehending and is often used in a manner not consistent with the rights of the ruler. M. Joseph Chailley,[2] a competent and impartial observer, whose book was revised in original and translated into English by Sir William Meyer, noticed this tendency, which he describes thus :

> The political officers who reside at their courts are in truth (I reproduce here native opinion which contains a material part but only a part of the truth) *their masters*.

[1] This restriction dates only from 1880.

[2] *Problems of British India*, by J. Chailley, Macmillan, 1910, p. 259.

> That may not be true in the case of the Nizam who has eleven million subjects nor perhaps in the state of Mysore with its five million; the opposition of rulers of this calibre might be inconvenient and they consequently escape from the annoying control of the political despot. But elsewhere the attitude of the political officer while ordinarily deferential in form (though even that is sometimes lacking) is the attitude of a servant who directs his nominal master, haughty, polite, impertinent and ironical. And what say the observers I am quoting are these political officers save spies whose words will be believed by the English in the face of all outside denial. Once they have pronounced a judgment on any matter, how can the chief appeal against it, save by the difficult and exceptional method of a letter to the Viceroy or a complaint to the Government and the peoples of the state are not deceived. They know their rulers are thus subject to masters and their attitude takes colour from this.

This picture, as M. Chailley himself points out, contains a material part of truth. All those who have direct experience of Indian states know that the whisper of the residency is the thunder of the state, and that there is no matter on which the Resident does not feel qualified to give advice. This method of unseen intervention is the ground of constant complaint and friction between the rulers and the Government, and there have been cases where Residents under a sense of pique or from anger resulting from legitimate opposition have visited princes and rulers with penalties for imaginary offences. The case of the Maharajah of Kashmir, whose first punishment had to be set aside later on, that of the ruler of Udaipur, whose letter to the Viceroy giving full details of his case, created a political scandal, that of the Rajah of Satara whose state was annexed on unproved accusations of the Resident, the high-handed policy of Colonel Macauley in Travancore, which led to military intervention, and numerous other instances well known in the history of Indian states, can be quoted in support of this.

The veiled dictatorship which has thus been the rule in Indian states has often been exercised through the agency of nominated ministers. That device lent itself admirably to the purposes of the Government. From the early days of the subsidiary alliance till to-day, it has been the main line of policy. Writing[1] in 1817, Sir Thomas Munro enunciated this policy with refreshing frankness in the following words. 'A subsidiary force would be a most useful establishment if it could be directed solely to the support of our ascendancy without nourishing all the vices of a bad government. But this seems to be almost impossible. The only way in which the object has ever been in any degree attained is by appointing a Dewan. The great difficulty is to prevent the prince from counteracting the Dewan and the Resident from meddling too much.' How far and how systematically this policy was carried out will be seen from the following incident described in Colonel Briggs' history of the Nizam.[2]

[1] *Wellesley Papers*, p. 795.
[2] Briggs' *Nizam*, p. 88.

> In this year (1804) occurred the death of Azeemul Omrah the Prime Minister, when the Nizam was strongly urged by the Resident to nominate Mir Alum to the vacant appointment. The Mir had long been known to be favourably inclined towards the British; and as the Nizam's disposition was sullen and discontented, and too fickle to be relied on, it was rightly judged that any advantage to be derived by the British from an alliance with the Hyderabad state depended in placing its resources under the control of a minister who should owe his elevation exclusively to their influence. . . .

Mir Alum was thus appointed Prime Minister, but there was a strong party against him at court. In order to support the minister who had thus been forced on the Nizam, the Resident had naturally to intervene decisively in all matters. The action taken by the Resident in order to get rid of all opposition to his creature best explains the situation. Mir Alum, on the pretext of paying a visit of condolence to the Resident, left the city and stayed with the Resident, when the latter compelled the Nizam to dismiss the opposition leaders, Ismail ee Yar Jung and Raja Mohiput Ram, from his court. Thereafter the minister returned to the city and took up his office as Prime Minister of the sovereign whom he had deserted, and even asked that a force should be detached for the protection of his person. After Mir Alum's death, the Resident procured the appointment of another of his nominees, Munir Ul Mulk. 'The real though not avowed object,' says Colonel Briggs, 'of the British resident through these negotiations was to effect an arrangement which, while it gave to the Nizam the appearance of having exercised his prerogative of appointing his own Dewan, *left the executive* in the hands of a minister who should be indebted to the resident alone for his elevation to power and feel that his maintenance in office depended solely on his subserviency to his wishes.' Matters went so far in the Nizam's court that when, during the administration of Chandu Lal, who took his orders from the Residency, the Nizam desired to ask him to furnish certain account, the Resident, Mr. Russell, considered it 'undue interference' in the duties of the minister.[1]

It may easily be imagined what the position was in other states when this was the condition of affairs in the premier state of India. In Gwalior the same tactics were followed. When Maharajah Junkoji Scindia died in 1843, Lord Ellenborough insisted on the election of one of his favourites as regent. On the favourite being expelled by the people of the state the Maharani was recognised as regent, but the governor would not recognise Dada Khasaji Walla as Dewan. In the case of Jodhpur the Maharajah was forced in 1868 to enter into an agreement by which it was laid down :

> If the Maharajah or the political agent considers the conduct of any minister such as to necessitate his dismissal or a vacancy occurs from any other cause a successor must be appointed by mutual consent. If an agreement

[1] Briggs' *Nizam*, p. 95.

on this point should not be possible, the successor should be decided by the Governor-General's agent who will give full consideration to His Highness's wishes.

In Cochin Dewan Sankara Warriyar was a tool in the hands of the Resident, whose clerk he was before becoming Dewan, and during the whole of his term he took his orders from the Resident and invited the British Government's intervention against his own Rajah.[1] From the time of the Travancore rebellion up to the time of Sir T. Madhava Rao, the Dewans of Travancore were invariably the nominees of the Resident, and generally clerks and other low officials who had served under him.

The relations between the Indian rulers and the Residents at their court have always been of a peculiar nature. Nominally advisers, the Residents, as M. Chailley points out, are really masters, and the treatment meted out by the Residents to the rulers has often been rude and extremely provocative. This was noticed by King Edward himself when he travelled in India as Prince of Wales. Writing to Queen Victoria on 14th November, 1875, the Prince said,[2] 'What struck me most forcibly was the rude and rough manner with which the English political officers (as they are called who are in attendance on native chiefs) treat them. It is indeed much to be deplored and the system is I am sure quite wrong.' Another English observer, Mr. Sidney Low, noticed the same thing. 'The Rajah,' says he, 'feels that

[1] *Cochin State Manual*, Ernakulam, 1911, pp. 170, 171.

[2] Sidney Lee, *Life of King Edward*, p. 399.

his brain is at least equal to that of a middle-aged middle-class colonel and he is quite aware that the diplomatist is nobody in particular when he goes back to his own country.'[1] The result is that things do not run smoothly, and there is always friction between the residency and the palace.

In more recent times the policy of the Government has been almost invariably to 'lend' British officials as Dewans, who naturally have their eyes on promotions in British India and on rewards in the form of British honours, and are inclined to look on the maintenance of British rights and the furtherance of European interests as their first duty. Until recently a large proportion of the high appointments in most states were held by loan officers of this kind, with the result that a peaceful penetration of British authority has been vigorously pushed forward.

The veiled dictatorship which the British Government exercises over the states shows itself also in the control of legislation and the authority reserved by the Government to hear direct petitions from the subjects of states. In most Indian states important legislation cannot be undertaken except with the previous sanction of the paramount power. In Cochin a religious endowment bill which was publicly announced and on which definite action was taken by the administration, had to be given up for refusal of sanction from the Government. The right of direct petition to the Viceroy, which the

[1] Sidney Low, *A Vision of India*, p. 136.

subjects of Indian states have begun freely to use against the rulers of their own states, is another invidious form of intervention which strikes at the root of the supposed independence of the states in internal administration.

Besides this normal method of intervention the British Government has usually looked upon minority administration as an opportunity for assuming or extending control. During temporary administration of this kind, extensive concessions used to be given to British companies, agreements were entered into for the alienating permanent rights, as in the case of Alwar and Bikaner, whose separate coinage was abolished at the time of the regency, and fundamental alterations of constitutions were undertaken as recently in Travancore where, under instructions from Simla, the Maharani was forced to separate religious administration from the general. The way was paved for encroachment and intervention. Gwalior, Jaipur, Mysore, Travancore, Baroda, Indore and most of the other states of India, felt at one time or other the effects of this method. Much resentment, naturally, has been aroused among the princes on this question. The Princes' Chamber in 1924 discussed very animatedly the limitation of the rights of regency administration to alienate state powers.

There are just and legitimate occasions of intervention both in the exercise of sovereign rights and for the purpose of maintaining a minimum standard of civilised government. Nor can it be questioned that in such matters as disputed succession, rebellion in the states, or the breakdown of law and order, the supreme Government has every right to step in. But the intervention of the Government of India, though on some occasions directed against the establishment of humane and just regulations or in support of popular rights as against the mis-government of a tyrannical chief, has often been undertaken in the interests of trade. The quarrel with Mir Kassim is well known. The Punjab Government threatened action against the Kashmir for not reducing certain duties which the state had imposed on articles that passed through Ladak. The secretary to the Government of the Punjab writing to the commissioner of Jullunder stated on behalf of the Government as follows : [1]

> But should His Highness the Maharajah fail to establish satisfactory arrangements at Ladak for the due encouragement of trade passing through that portion of his territory the Lieutenant Governor will be quite prepared to recommend to the supreme government that a British Officer of rank and position be stationed at Ladak for a season.

Intervention is sometimes undertaken rather for the political advantage or the trade interests of the British than in the interests of the people or the state. Lord William Bentinck as Governor of Madras wrote to Lord Wellesley that the ' exigencies of the Rajah of Travancore ' afforded a favourable

[1] Letter from T. H. Thornton, Secretary to the Government of the Punjab, to T. D. Forsyth, C.B., Commissioner of Jullunder, No. 827, dated 1860, quoted in Lucullus Kashmere Raj.

opportunity for intervention with a view to modifying the subsidiary alliance. It is intervention of this kind that has made the rulers of Indian states look upon Residents not as friendly advisers but as hostile agents against whom one has to be on guard. It is the same knowledge that has made all malcontents in the state look upon the agent of the British Government as the person to appeal to over the head of their own ruler. For the unpopularity of the Resident in Indian states this false historical tradition is responsible.

As a result, no doubt, of the organisation of Princes for common action, the attitude of the Government with regard to intervention in the purely internal affairs of the state has changed considerably. The differentiation between sovereign and non-sovereign states—those in which the policy of intervention is expressly repudiated in treaties and those in which it is authorised—has been emphasised. This differentiation, as we have shown, is historical but, as Lord Chelmsford himself recognised, it has been forgotten. The attempt to class states enjoying full rights of internal management with minor states which have no criminal jurisdiction and the rulers of which have undertaken loyally to obey the advices given by the Resident has been fruitful of much trouble. The determination of the extent of legitimate intervention in states can only be made on the basis of this fundamental difference. A codification of practice would then be possible, and the Government of India would be freed from the accusation now made freely and with justice, that neither the express stipulation of the treaty nor the solemn assurance of the sovereign of Britain could guarantee the Princes of India against undue and unauthorised interference from the political department.

VIII

THE RIGHTS OF SOVEREIGNTY

THE question as to whether Indian states are sovereign, and if so, to what extent and in what manner, is one that is of more than academical interest. Its discussion is necessitated primarily by the fact that the Austinian conception of sovereignty as indivisible and unitary has so far held the field in politics and denied from the constitutional and theoretical point of view the right of Indian states to be called sovereign. Accepting the Austinian definition, that the sovereign is the superior who enforces and receives obedience and who yields obedience to none, and, ignoring some of the facts of political life, Anglo-Indian jurists have declared Indian states to be non-sovereign communities. If it is accepted as a principle that sovereignty is indivisible and that only the power that is legally omnicompetent can claim that authority, then the conclusion naturally follows that Indian states are no more sovereign than either trade unions or dissenting churches. To this constitutional theory official opinion has given some political support as when Lord Curzon declared in the Bhawalpur speech, that 'the sovereignty of the crown is everywhere unchallenged. It has itself laid down the limitations of its own prerogative.'[1] Again in the circular, No. 1700 E, 21st August, 1891, the Government of India officially declared that the paramount supremacy of Her Majesty presupposes and implies the subordination of Indian rulers. This comprehensive claim on behalf of the British Government and the implied denial of sovereign rights to Indian rulers are clear proofs of the influence of the Austinian conception of sovereignty in Indian political thought. The actual fact of political experience in India that the people of Indian states accept as their sovereign only the rulers themselves is explained away by declaring that the Crown itself has laid down the limitation of its prerogatives. This explanation could be used, clearly, to justify any claim. The Chinese Republic, for example, may declare itself to be the unchallenged sovereign of Hong Kong or Spain of Gibraltar, or England of Normandy, with the necessary addition that 'the Crown has merely laid down the limitation of its own prerogative.' It is clear that the Austinian idea of sovereignty would not fit in with the political facts of India's case. Those who in the interests of a dogma attempt to find ingenious explanations would be driven to the same methods as those by which Le Fur has attempted to preserve the form of the omnicompetent state even in the theory of Federalism.

The sovereign power of modern law is, in reality,

[1] *Curzon in India*, p. 227.

a fictitious leviathan, the curious outcome of a combination of royal power with Roman *imperium*, to which, as the medieval king was also a feudal lord, was added the conception of allegiance and ownership. Bodin, Hobbes, de Loholme and others, the alchemists who transmuted these conceptions into the modern conception of sovereignty, were interested in the deification of the state's power. But at no time and in no country did the theory approximate to political facts. The British Parliament in the plenitude of its power declared that no Catholic in Ireland was worth more than five pounds, but that does not seem to have either materially impoverished the Catholics there or made their property purchasable for that sum. Bismarck declared that he would not go to Canossa, but the humiliation which awaited the Austinian experiment was greater than that which followed the physical submission of the Emperor. When Lloyd George invited de Valera to send his delegates, the Austinian sovereign had to be conveniently forgotten or relegated to be honoured only in academic discussions. The theory of undivided sovereignty, in fact, died an inglorious death more than six hundred years ago when Nogaret rode into Anagni and arrested him who had declared not in conceit but with conviction, 'I am Caesar, I am Pope.' All the legist attempts to resuscitate that theory can no more be successful than the attempt of all the king's horses and all the king's men to put Humpty Dumpty back on the wall.

The modern attempt to bring this conception

actually into the life of states, apart from the sterile field of scholastic discussion, dates from the French constitution of 1791, which declared that 'sovereignty is one indivisible, inalienable and imprescriptible.' But with all the force of the great revolution and Napoleon behind her, France has not so far been able to carry out this view into practice, and the claim of regionalism is probably greater to-day in France than at any time since the fall of the Girondins. But almost side by side with this assertion by revolutionary France of the conception of undivided sovereignty, there was growing up in America from roots implanted from the Netherlands the idea of the state as a complex of rights and authorities which is the essence of federalism. As M. Duguit points out, federalism is essentially constituted on the basis 'that there exists on the same territory only one nation but several states invested as such with sovereign power. Every federation is divided into a central and federal state which is the nation regarded as a state, and local groups, themselves states, constitute the federation.' [1]

The writers who are anxious to fit facts to theory rather than theory to facts have striven to deny sovereignty either to the central organisation or to the constituent states. Some, like Dicey, have denied sovereignty to the constituent bodies, while others, like Seydel, have gone to the extent of declaring that the central authority even in the

[1] Leon Duguit, *Law in the Modern State*, George Allen & Unwin, 1921.

German Empire is not sovereign. The easy solution that there can be non-sovereign states is obviously untenable, because in all modern states, including the great powers, there is a very strict limitation of authority by international agreement and very definite rights of interference from outside bodies. So, between a state like China, bound hand and foot by international agreements, and a great power like England, the difference is one of degree rather than of principle.

The difficulty is mainly a result of attempting to maintain a theory that cannot explain the facts of politics. The undivided sovereign of the Austinian school is a meaningless metaphysical conception. Sovereignty is divisible, and in all modern states this principle is frankly admitted. Sovereignty is, after all, the complex of public powers, and its division is not only possible but constantly undertaken in the relation between states. The real basis of the conception of sovereignty is that contained in Cardinal Newman's phrase, ' degrees of obedience ' ; and when co-ordinate obedience to different sources of public power in different matters is possible, it is clear that sovereignty is divided and shared between them.

In India the sovereignty of the bigger states is unimpeachable. Their courts of law are supreme ; legally the ultimate source of authority is vested in them. Many states have their own coinage. The persons of their rulers are inviolable and above law. They have, by law, absolute rights of life and property over their subjects. These are not rights derived from the British Government, though the British Government has guaranteed them in exchange for the surrender of certain other rights. True, they have no independent international status in the sense that they can neither accredit nor receive ministers. This limits their external independence, but cannot be said to affect their sovereignty in matters in which by treaty they still possess full and final authority. Till 1920 Afghanistan had not the right of direct diplomatic relationship with other states, but the sovereignty of the Amir was a fact which even the strongest claimants of British imperialism could not have denied. It is only on the basis that there can be degrees of sovereignty and that sovereign authority is divisible that these facts could be explained or understood.

The Government itself has come officially to this point of view. The basis of discussion of the constitution of the Princes' Chamber was that the Chamber should be composed of 'the ruling princes of India exercising full *sovereign powers*, *i.e.* unrestricted civil and criminal jurisdiction over their subjects and the power to make their own laws.' Thus, according to the princes themselves, 'full sovereign powers meant the right to make their own laws and unrestrained civil and criminal jurisdiction.' It is also implied that there may be degrees of sovereignty and jurisdiction and that there are among the Indian rulers varying degrees of sovereign authority.

It is quite true that for purposes of international law these states have ceased to be independent and sovereign. On that question there is not the least doubt. But so far as internal sovereignty is concerned it is equally clear that their prerogatives and authority, and the loyalty which their subjects owe to them, admit of no dispute and are inherent in their own rights and not derivative from an outside source. The recognised outward symbols of sovereignty, such as the right to give titles, to have coins and stamps, to be inviolable and above law, to have the authority to promulgate legislation which commands unquestioned obedience, the major Indian states possess and are guaranteed in their possession by treaties. They give titles of honour and distinction to their own subjects. The Nizam gives the title of Maharajah, Rajah, Nawab, Dewan and all the rest of the recognised Indian titles of honour. His right to give titles to British subjects has been denied, but that in no way interferes with his own right as the fountain of honour for his own subjects. The chief maharajahs all over India enjoy this right, and everywhere this is considered an exclusive prerogative of sovereignty.

Full powers of civil and criminal justice are also enjoyed by the independent rulers. They have their own High Courts from which there is no appeal either to the Privy Council or to the King. The right of appeal, if reserved at all, is reserved to the ruler himself, and in some states the Maharajah exercises this function through a Ministry of Appeal as in the case of Gwalior. As the fountain of justice the 'full-powered' rulers in India are uncontrolled masters of life and property, and most of them could declare with greater truth than Richard II that law was in their breasts. They have the right of legislation, which they exercise either personally or, as in the case of Mysore, Cochin or Travancore, through a legislative council empowered to originate, discuss and pass legislation with the consent of the ruler. The councils derive their authority entirely from the ruler, and are answerable to none but him. The laws thus made are enforced with all the authority of the sovereign, and all who owe allegiance to the ruler and those whose nationality do not give the right of trial by their own countrymen have to obey them like any other law. Disobedience is visited with penalties exactly in the same way as in other sovereign states.

The inviolability of the ruler's person and the powerlessness of courts not only in his own state but even in British India and elsewhere to try him or punish him are well-understood facts. In the case of Statham *v.* Statham and the Gaekwar of Baroda it was laid down that the courts in England can have no jurisdiction over an Indian ruling prince. Extraordinary commissions have on occasions tried Indian princes, as in the case of Malhar Rao Gaekwar, who was publicly tried before an extraordinary tribunal. There is no doubt that the Government exceeded its powers in this matter, for though there have been worse examples of misrule and disloyalty since then, no single ruler has been tried in public. The mere fact that an action exceeding recognised powers has been taken would not constitute a precedent. An English court tried and executed Mary of Scotland, who was an independent ruler, but that precedent does not create a right for the British Crown to try and excute the crowned sovereigns of foreign countries. Malhar Rao Gaekwar's trial was certainly unconstitutional, and the weakness of the Indian rulers in demanding their just rights is the only reason why it took place. The case of the Jubraj of Manipur was different, as he was only the heir apparent; and what was done in his case was done as an act of war, almost in the same way as the execution of Charles I by Parliament. These cases do not give the paramount power a right nor take away from the princes the inviolability of their persons or their prerogative of being above the law of their own state, or laws promulgated by the British Government for the observance of its subjects.

The right to have coins and stamps, which is another equally valued symbol of sovereignty, is enjoyed by the major Indian states. Hyderabad has a whole system of coinage, and other states also enjoy it in varying degrees. The states that have separate inland postage have their own stamps, as in the case of Cochin.

Military establishments varying from considerable forces of fighting value to a few men in uniform are the universal characteristic of Indian states. As we have seen, in Hyderabad, Gwalior, Indore, Bikanir, Patiala and other states the armies are effective units, besides being the insignia of sovereignty. But everywhere the rulers look upon their military establishment as demonstrating their right to maintain an independent force, which is an important part of sovereignty The limitation of armaments does not necessarily take away the sovereignty of a state, as by the treaty of Paris Russia was forced to limit her naval armaments in the Black Sea, and by the recent European settlement Germany and the enemy powers are under obligation to disarm.

The theoretical sovereignty, therefore, of Indian rulers who enjoy full powers within their state, cannot be denied. It must also be pointed out, however, that the gradation of sovereignty in the case of the smaller princelings of Kathiawad and Bundlekund and the Simla states, who are merely mediatised chiefs rather than rulers, vanishes almost to the point of nothingness. Their position has little in common with that of the independent states, though they also enjoy rights and privileges such as belonged to feudal lords in medieval Europe.

The rigid theory which turned the sovereign into a legal and metaphysical abstraction, and invested him with powers which no human institution can possess over others, has gone the way of other abstractions that have forgotten the facts. The juristic theory of an absolute final and undivided authority has had no historical experience to back it. The most obvious facts of national organisation such as co-ordinate states in federalism, the international position of the Irish Free State and the Dominions in the British Empire, the peculiar position of Bavaria and Saxony in Germany, and those of the Indian states in relation to the Central Government, had to be ignored or distorted to suit a theory which had nothing in its favour but a logical symmetry. The only acceptable theory of sovereignty is that of a complex of public powers which could in its permutation and combination vary from the full-powered international state like England or Japan to one like Baroda or Mysore where the ruler has internationally no independent status but enjoys sovereign powers within his own territory. Unless we come back to the truth emphasised by Sir Henry Maine that sovereignty is essentially divisible, we are likely to be misled by the conflict of jurisdiction to the utterly wrong conclusion that the Indian states have no rights except those given by the will and pleasure of the British Government, that the rulers of Indian states are rulers by the grace of the King Emperor and not of their own rights. That would be a position justified neither by history nor by the known facts of the case. There can be no doubt that within the limits set by the agreements that define their relation with the British Government Indian rulers are sovereigns by every criterion of political science.

IX

THE CONSTITUTIONAL POSITION

THE relation between the Government of India and the princes, though mainly based on treaties, is governed by certain obvious political and legal considerations which may be called the conventions of our constitution. Without a proper understanding of these the position of the states cannot be fully realised. During the course of the last century and a quarter, these relations have undergone such changes that a mere reading of the treaties would give an altogether false impression of the position. A collection of principles threatening to become by precedent, interpretation and analogy a separate system of public law has been developed; and the procedure of the political department is as complicated as it is varied. An analysis of the conventions and principles underlying the relations is necessary if we are to avoid the pitfall of taking too rigid and too legal an attitude on this question.

At the outset it should be remembered that the Government of India is not only the successor of the East India Company which made treaties on the basis of equality with Indian princes, but also the trustee and representative of the wider interests of the country. The fact that it is the *British* Government should not obscure the other fact that it is the Government of India, while the states are only fragments historically and politically marked off on the map. It is this fact that has been very clumsily and objectionably described when it was claimed that the British Government not only represented the Company but was, so to say, the testamentary successor of the Moghul Empire. In whatever way it is expressed, there can be no denying the fact that on the Government of India falls the duty of seeing that the rights of the Indian states are not used against, and in their effects do not become detrimental to, the general welfare of India. The broad interests of the whole of India cannot fail to be of equal interest to the states also; and hence, this limitation is, in the larger view, no encroachment on the rights of the states but a safeguarding of their position. Thus, there has arisen a vast body of agreements beyond the scope of the treaties which govern the relations of the states with the Government. Nevertheless, the most important basis of the complicated polity that has arisen is the treaty which binds each state to the Government. The word 'treaty' in legal as well as in common language is used only for the most solemn agreements between independent nations. A treaty is presumed to be a voluntary act on both sides, and a breach of it can be punished only by the use of force and not by an appeal to a court of law. All treaties are above the jurisdiction of ordinary law, and failure to observe a condition can be visited only by the penalties prescribed in the treaty itself. A repudiation of the treaty can only be met with the sanctions that uphold the agreement. Even in the case of the Sultan of Johore in Mighell *v.* the Sultan of Johore, a sovereign whose position is similar to that of the Indian princes, it was held that the treaty which bound him not to enter into any engagement with any foreign state was 'not an abnegation of his right to enter into such treaties, but only a condition upon which the protection stipulated for is to be given. If the Sultan disregards it, the consequences may be the loss of that protection or possibly other difficulties with this country.'[1] It may be sufficient cause for hostile action on the side of the other contracting party which may lead to the annexation of the country and the deprivation of the ruler's right. But the essence of a treaty is that its breach cannot be punished by law as its sanction does not rest on the municipal law of the country. Thus the failure to respect treaty obligations led to hostilities in the case of Coorg and to forcible intervention in the recent case of Nabha, where the Maharajah violated the sovereignty of Patiala and in other ways ignored treaty obligations.

The relationship, however, as has been pointed out, is not entirely based on treaty. Considerations of all-Indian interest, conventions regarding sovereign authority, agreements in connection with customs, etc., such as the inter-portal convention with

[1] J. B. Scott, *Cases of International Law*, p. 284.

Travancore and Cochin and other rights either surrendered by the Indian states or accepted tacitly by rulers, supplement the original restrictions contained in the treaty. There results from this an implied or clearly understood legal bond. There is no right of secession, because the states are internal states and their right by treaty is clearly limited by the wider consideration of the interests of India. If they have no right of secession, they can have no right to declare war, and obligations of this nature effectively restricting the operation of treaty rights constitute an important factor in the relations of Indian states.

It must, however, be understood that these relations are altogether extra-constitutional, and the bond that unites is in no way the claim of the paramount power to a feudal sovereignty. The Indian rulers have consistently repudiated the feudal theory which was sought to be foisted upon them. A large number of the states of Kathiawad, Bundlekund and the Simla hills are undoubtedly feudatory, for their relations with the sovereign from whom their allegiance was transferred were of that kind. Thus, the chiefs of the Mahikanta Agency were petty tributaries of the Gaekwar, and the southern Mahratta Jagirdars were no more than officials of the Peishwa. But the feudal tie is not binding on states possessing independent treaty rights, and the attempt of the political department from the time of Lord Canning to that of Lord Curzon to interpret the relationship in the terms of the feudal king and his lords cannot be justified either from history of from fact. The assumption of the imperial title and the system of Durbars which followed it were in part the outcome and in part the cause of this feudal misconception, which the princes have never accepted. They have attended the Durbars under protest, and have always considered the compulsion to attend it as an unjust use of *force majeure*. The feudal tie is personal, while in India the rights of Indian princes are in relation to the Government of India and only indirectly to the King Emperor.

The most obvious fact in the complex system of the relations between Indian states and the Government is that they form one definite Indian polity—the Indian Empire. Internationally British India together with the states forms one unity. Even as regards the British Empire, India, both British as well as Indian, is a single entity. The disabilities which Indian subjects suffer in the colonies extend to the subjects of the princes. The rights which Indian subjects possess elsewhere are enjoyed by the subjects of the princes. The states form part of the political system. There are evident both in the system and in the relationship which is the basis of it important elements of a federal tie. The whole theory of federalism is that while the constituents remain sovereign and independent the claims of the Central Government are recognised in a definite surrender of certain important rights. That is the essence, beyond a doubt, of the Indian system, so far as it relates to the major states. The joint political entity of the states and British India is recognised, and the Government of India as the Central Government exercises certain rights which the states have surrendered. The tie is thus essentially federal and is based on a division of sovereignty. It is not a confederation, because the right to secede does not exist, and the Central Government has become the only authority responsible for defence and high policy. The federalism of Indian polity is, of course, much more limited, inasmuch as the Central Government has practically no legislative, executive or fiscal authority over the states. It is true that the jurisdiction of European and American residents is reserved for it, and that the Central Government through its own executive officers controls the telegraph and postal systems which operate even within the limits of the states. But that can be considered only as a part of the action taken for defence. The Central Government as vested in the Governor-General in Council has no powers of legislation which would, without the express enactment of the rulers, affect the subjects of states. This and other restrictions only show that the federalism that has developed in the imperial polity of India is of a weak and to some extent inchoate character, but that fundamentally the system is a federalism no one who has examined the facts can deny. The federal system of Germany, though it preserves the independence of the states and preserved the sovereignty of the rulers, gave to the empire authority for legislation, fiscal policy, judicial administration, besides full authority for the control of foreign policy involving the right of declaring war and concluding peace. The federal tie was so strengthened that advocates of the unitary state, such as Treitschke, declared that the Empire, though federal in form, was unitary in fact. In India, while the federal principle has been recognised in the right of the Government to sole control in questions of defence, and the acceptance by the rulers of the right of Government to build telegraph lines and maintain a postal system within the territories of the states under imperial officers, the independence of the princes has remained unchallenged. Those rights which were clearly contrary to the fundamental conception of the federal principle, as the right to denounce the treaty and to secede, have vanished, while in their place the princes have obtained the privilege of discussing in the Princes' Chamber affairs common to their territories and to British India. The federal idea, while it has necessarily restricted their independence in those matters, such as defence, that are vested in the Central Government, has given to those princes who possess sovereign rights the duties of the constituent states of a federal body. It is only in this line that the polity of India can develop, for the future Indian Empire can only be a union of states. As His Highness the Maharajah of Alwar declared, 'My goal is the "United States of India" where every province, every state working out its own destiny, in accordance with its own environment, its tradition, history and religion, will combine together for higher and imperial purposes, each subscribing its little quota of knowledge and experience in a labour of love freely given for a noble and higher cause.'

X

THE FUTURE

WITH the introduction of the Montagu-Chelmsford reforms and the institution of the Princes' Chamber, the position of the Indian states has undergone a subtle though important change. The establishment of the Princes' Chamber is in itself a departure. It meant the surrender of one of the most cherished principles of British policy in relation to the Indian states, viz. the refusal to permit joint action, or interest in each other's affairs. A community of interest alone can be the basis of a political organisation, and the Government of India in convoking a permanent body constituted of the ruling princes tacitly accepted the right of each one of them to be interested in the welfare of the whole and to work for the interests of the entire body.

The idea underlying this change was thus defined by the authors of the Reforms Report :

> We wish to call into existence a permanent consultative body. There are questions which affect the states generally or other questions which are of concern either to the Empire as a whole or to British India and the states in common upon which we conceive the opinion of such a body would be of the utmost value. . . . Any member

> of the council or the council as a whole might request the Viceroy to include in its agenda any subject on which discussion is desired. . . . The direct transaction of business between the Government and any state would of course not be affected by the institution of the council.

The King's proclamation of 1921 at its inauguration again defined its limits.

> My Viceroy will take its counsel freely in matters relating to the territories of Indian states generally and in matters that affect these territories jointly with British India or with the rest of my Empire. It will have no concern with the internal affairs of individual states or their rulers or with the relations of individual states with my Government while the existing rights of these states and their freedom of action will in no way be prejudiced or impaired.

The purpose of the Princes' Chamber and its limited scope are thus clearly defined. As a consultative body concerned with affairs relating to princes, it constitutes a great advance in the relations of the princes with the Central Government. By belonging to it no state loses its independence or right of direct negotiation, and the internal affairs of no state can be discussed unless the ruler himself desires it. Further, the princes of India as a body gain the right of discussing affairs which are of concern either to the Empire as a whole or to British India and the states in common. The value of the Chamber and its influence on the relation of the Government of India are to be seen in the modification of the arbitrary methods so far pursued by the political department in relation to the states.

The very first question that attracted the attention of the princes was the codification of political practice. Speaking at the first session of the Chamber, Lord Chelmsford said :

> The next recommendation is that with the consent of the rulers of states their relations with the Government of India should be examined not necessarily with a view to any change of policy but in order to simplify, standardise and codify existing practice for the future. In his journal written more than a hundred years ago Lord Hastings referred to the formidable mischief which has arisen from our not having defined to ourselves or made clear to the Native Princes the quality of the relations which we have established with them. In the memorandum prepared in January last by a committee of Your Highnesses this sentence is quoted with approval. I realise that the memorandum must not be taken as conveying the considered opinion of those who did not share in its preparation and I believe that with regard to this proposal also some concern has been felt by some among your number lest standardisation should involve a diminution of treaty rights. . . .
>
> On the other hand, although direct agreement naturally constitutes the most important source of obligations existing between the British Government and the states, yet it does not supply the full basis and the study of long established custom, and practice is essential to a proper comprehension of the true character of the bond. The Government of India are anxious that the matter should be most fully ventilated because the suggestion has been made that custom and practice have in the past tended to encroach in certain respects on treaty rights. . . . I shall welcome any general observations which any of Your Highnesses may desire to make during the conference

either on the subject of infringement of treaty rights or in regard to the possibility of revising treaties or simplifying or standardising custom and practice. There is an obvious risk that any over rigid standardisation might fail to take due account of the peculiar circumstances of particular states and of the special obligations which we owe to them by treaty. But the advantages of a cautious codification are also clear and the tendency of all progress is towards greater definition. Of recent years we have endeavoured to review our practice under various heads. It is possible that many of Your Highnesses may consider that if the recommendations made in the remaining items of the agenda are eventually adopted and especially the recommendation in regard to placing the important states in direct political relations with the Government of India, the desired unification of practice and development of constitutional doctrines will follow.[1]

In fact, on such questions as minority administration and succession procedure much has already been done in the nature of establishing well-defined practice. This has more than brought out and re-established the fact that the rights of Indian states are inherent and not dependent on the 'grace' of His Majesty, as Lord Curzon and others had tried to assert. The Princes' Chamber does not in any way interfere either with the internal independence of the state or with its right to maintain direct relations with the Government of India. What it does is in fact to maintain the claim that the rights, jurisdictions and authorities of the sovereign princes of India are based on treaties and political practice arising out of mutual agreement,

[1] *Lord Chelmsford's Speeches*, p. 159 *et seq.*

to alter which the consent of both the parties is required.

The establishment of the Princes' Chamber has also helped to emphasise the difference which the political department had conveniently tried to forget as the Montagu-Chelmsford Report itself admits —between the sovereign and non-sovereign states in India. Sir John Malcolm, Sir Charles Metcalfe and all others who shaped Anglo-Indian policy in an earlier generation recognised this. Wellesley recognised it when he drew attention to the difficulties arising from relations with independent states in his Mysore despatch, and meant the treaty with Mysore to be a model for the new system of subsidiary alliances. Sir Charles Metcalfe in 1837 classified the Indian states into 'quasi' sovereign states and dependent principalities. The Marquis of Dalhousie's policy in relation to the important question of adoption was based on the differentiation between dependent vassal states and sovereign rulers. The Montagu-Chelmsford Report recognises the difference and admits that it has been lost sight of when it says, 'that practice appropriate to the minor chiefs has been used even in the case of the major ones.'

This differentiation is all-important in the question of Indian states. To jumble together in the same category sovereign princes enjoying rights of life and death, ruling over millions of people and maintaining military establishments and independent administration, like Hyderabad, Gwalior, Baroda, Mysore and Travancore, with the petty princelings of a few villages, is indeed to hide facts under a false nomenclature. From the point of view of administrative independence the states should be classified under three heads: those that have complete legislative and executive independence within their borders, those that have it partially and under effective supervision, and those that do not have it. Only the first two classes have salutes, but even among them it is necessary that a clear distinction should be made. The third class, which makes up by far the largest number, should cease to be classed as Indian states, and should be declared to be feudatories with special honours and jurisdictions. Such, evidently, is the present tendency; and the exclusion of such states from the Princes' Chamber would hasten the clear demarcation of the class. The rights of the first class are guaranteed to them by treaty, and the Government of India cannot but withdraw from the false position it has taken up in identifying them with the minor chiefs. Their position is clear, and can only be strengthened by the establishment of such an institution as the Princes' Chamber.

It is only with regard to the second class of princes that serious difficulty arises. In their case generally there is expressly reserved a right of intervention in internal affairs, supervision of criminal jurisdiction and in some cases limitation of judicial authority and restriction of the right of legislation, and farther, as in the case of Kolhapur, the reservation of residuary rights for the British

Government. These states are sovereign only in a more limited way than the others.

The Princes' Chamber has also helped the states to maintain the undoubted residuary rights they possess in matters not mentioned in the treaty. Thus, for example, the question of wireless and aerial transport which ten years ago would have been considered to belong entirely to the province of the Central Government, is now a subject of common discussion in the Chamber. Though in some cases the Central Government has reserved for itself the residuary rights not mentioned in the agreement, it is clear enough that in most of the treaties with Indian states the rulers have surrendered only those rights which are mentioned in the treaty itself. The benefit of any omissions must go to them, as they are presumed to have been in full sovereign authority at the time of the treaty. This does not affect, of course, the minor chiefs like the southern Mahratta Jaghirdars, or the chiefs of Kathiawad. But it is an obvious fact with regard to sovereign states. Though the Government itself has never denied this fact or challenged the rights of princes developing in new directions in internal affairs, yet on questions which it considered to affect imperial policy the Government claimed the benefit of a constructive interpretation and sometimes actually put forward claims in virtue of its sovereign position—an attempt, in fact, to claim residuary authority in certain matters. Thus, for example, the Government of India has reserved for itself the right of telegraphic construction, though on the basis of treaties with Indian states no such valid claim could be made. Such encroachments are now less easy to make, for the Princes' Chamber is fully alive to this question and has, in fact, set up committees to discuss how a common wireless policy and encouragement of aerial navigation could be undertaken, subjects which would have been purely imperial some time ago.

The position of the states in the British Empire as a separate constituent of it has also been recognised. The King's proclamation said that the Viceroy was to consult them in matters affecting their territories jointly with British India or *with the rest of the Empire*. Thus, the princes have gained a new status as autonomous sovereign states not of the Indian Empire only but of the *British* Empire. The Indian delegation to the Imperial Conference always included a ruling prince as representative of the independent states of India. The admission of princes to the League of Nations has been not on the basis of their being rulers of Indian states, about whom international law knows nothing, but of their being members of the Indian delegation.

The Indian princes, moreover, have gained the right of discussing major problems of policy in British India, such as defence, legislation that may affect them, *e.g.* in tariff matters, without the Indian legislature obtaining any corresponding rights in their affairs. Their collective opinion with regard to political reforms in India is known to carry great weight with the authorities. Thus, while preserving their absolute internal independence and, indeed, strengthening it by a revision of treaties and agreements and the codification of political practice, the princes have gained a new position as Indian and imperial personalities who have collectively a right to be consulted on matters affecting policy and whose voice naturally carries great weight. They have been, in fact, collectively recognised as an independent constituent of the Empire.

There can be no doubt that this is the only line of true development for the princes. While the minor chiefs become noblemen of position with certain special rights and take their place in Indian society, the major rulers will have their independence confirmed while gaining a new position as partners in the wider commonwealth. The true ideal of a future Indian polity can only thus be kept in view, for a united India can no more ignore the princes than the princes can ignore British India which surrounds them on every side. The only future that can be visualised for India is as a congeries of internally autonomous states united together under a strong central Government which would look after their common interests. For such a consummation the present line of development, in which the Indian princes while strengthened in their independence take their place also as sons of India owing a duty to the common country, is undeniably the right one.

APPENDIX I

NOTE I

Kathiawad Agency

The peculiar polity of Kathiawad, which stands midway between independent rulers and mediatised chiefs, requires to be studied separately. The body of public and private law which is there current is entirely different from that of British India and that of the regular Indian states. Relations with the British Government also stand on a different footing.

The whole area of the Kathiawad agency, 20,882 square miles, comprises no less than 143 states. Of these only fourteen states have any kind of final jurisdiction, seven of them (Junagadh, Navnagar, Bhawnagar, Porbandar, Dharangdhara Morvi and Gondal) being classed as first-class states enjoying sovereign attributes. Seven others, including Limbdi and Rajkote, have more limited powers, but enjoy jurisdiction over their own subjects.

This complicated system arose from the accidents of historical growth. Both the Peishwa and the Gaekwar claimed sovereign rights over the Kathiawad area. The amounts due to them from the local chieftains were collected by the Mulkgiri system, under which an annual military expedition was sent to get the recognised payments. By the Treaty of 1805 with the Gaekwar, the British Government guaranteed that potentate's rights over Kathiawad, but soon discovered that in undertaking to maintain the Gaekwar's supremacy it was lending its authority to perpetuate a system of devastating military expeditions, which was neither fruitful in political results nor in conformity with recognised principles of orderly government. The Gaekwar was then advised to make agreements with these princes and to take from them fixed money payments, while leaving the chiefs full autonomy. Accordingly, a settlement was made with 153 states by Instruments known as Fael Zamin, by which the chief undertook to remain peaceful and pay the contributions which were therein fixed. This document also laid the responsibility for maintaining public peace on the chiefs. As a result of the conflicting jurisdictions and long-established family and clan feuds, Kathiawad had been a prey to the most terrible confusion in which public order depended on the will, caprice or strength of arm of the 153 chiefs among whom the area was partitioned. By the Fael Zamin each chief undertook not to molest merchants and travellers, not to attack or quarrel with his neighbours, and provided another chief to guarantee for his fulfilment of the conditions. The rights of the Mahratta powers were continued, but in 1817 the Peishwa ceded what belonged to him to the British Government. The Gaekwar's right to send troops and collect revenues direct was also given up in 1820, when the British Government undertook to collect and pay to the Gaekwar the tributes owing to his Government. Since then the British Government has been in the position of the sole sovereign. This position carried with it the right of judicial interference which the Gaekwar had enjoyed, and on that basis a criminal court of justice presided over by the Agent was established in 1831.

A political settlement determining administrative and judicial problems was effected in 1866. As the powers, privileges and authorities of the chiefs were undefined, and led naturally to chaos, the Government had to intervene in order to determine the exact nature of the relationships in which these states stood to one another and to the British Government. The whole area was divided into four regions or 'prants,' over each of which a British political officer holding judicial and magisterial powers was appointed. The chiefs themselves were classified, and their powers defined.

The main difficulty of the political system of Kathiawad is the right of partition belonging to certain minor states and ruling families. The subdivision of possessions has gone to such an extent that in some cases chieftainships extend to no more than one or two villages. Hence Kathiawad has become a veritable museum of petty sovereignties.

Whether or not the minor Kathiawad states enjoy any inherent right to be considered different from British India is a controversial question. It is certain that neither the Peishwa nor the Gaekwar considered these tracts as being in possession of sovereign rights, and that they reserved for themselves the authority to intervene and to act as they chose. But the British Government, in standing forth as the sole sovereign, disclaimed all such pretensions. As Sir Henry Maine in his famous memorandum on this subject has pointed out,[1] the rights inherited from the Peishwa and the Gaekwar, have never been actively asserted, the Court of Directors having in fact declared in 1830 that they had no idea of enforcing those claims. It is clear, however, that they stand on a different footing, as the states have no clearly defined treaty rights, but those which are expressly granted to them. As Sir Henry Maine expressed it, though the states are in enjoyment of several sovereign rights, 'by far the largest part of sovereign rights has obviously resided in practice with the British Government, and among the rights it has exercised appears to me an almost unlimited

[1] *Sir Henry Maine, A Brief Memoir*, by the Right Honourable Sir M. E. Grant Duff, with some of his Indian Speeches; John Murray, 1892, p. 321.

interference for the better order of the states.' The position has considerably changed with regard to the first-class states which by their size, importance and progressive character, have acquired the status almost similar to those of treaty states elsewhere. These like Nawanagar are members of the Princes' Chamber, and though historically of the same origin as the rest may now be classed with the sovereign states.

NOTE II

The Mediatised States

The mediatised states which form the strictly feudatory portion of the Indian states, constitute an order by themselves whose prerogatives, privileges and political rights differ fundamentally from those of the sovereign states. Their inclusion in the category of Indian states has been the cause of much confusion. The mediatised states are the domains of chiefs who were or are themselves dependent on other rulers but whose position and rights have been guaranteed by the British Government. The problem first arose in Malwa and Bundelkand.[1] When Malwa and Central India were pacified there existed a large number of petty chiefs tributary to the great Mahratta states like Gwalior and Indore. The British Government, while guaranteeing nominal sovereign rights to these suzerain states, limited their exercise and undertook to maintain the autonomy and rights of the minor chiefs from encroachment from their erstwhile sovereigns. Such guaranteed chiefs are of two classes, those in whose administration the sovereign ruler is expressly excluded from interference, as Ratlam, and others who have no such guarantee, as Bagli. In the case of the former their succession and adoption have to be recognised only by the British Government, and the sovereign ruler

[1] Aitchison, vol. iv. p. 2.

has no right of intervention. In the case of the latter the sovereign chief has a right to be heard about legitimacy and directness of descent. In the case of Bagli the adoption of Raghu nath Singh was questioned by Scindia in 1866, but the British Government held it to be valid.

No mediatised chiefs have power of life and death, and their civil and criminal jurisdiction is exercised under the supervision of the political agent. They have no rights of a residuary nature, and their authority is strictly limited to what is expressly granted.

It is also important to realise the position of the mediatised chiefs who have an intermediate sovereign like Sikar, Khehtri, and other Rajputana chiefs, and those like the southern Mahratta Jaghirdars whose intermediary sovereign —the Peishwa—ceased to exist long ago. The position of these states, such as those of Bundelkand, Kathiawad and the Simla Hills, materially differs from that of the ruling princes. These territories are held not by virtue of direct treaties but as a result of settlement with a superior, by a system of general pacification. The Mahikanta agency, which contains so many minor rulers, was under the sovereignty of the Gaekwar and was taken over by agreement with him, and the states in the agency have only those rights which are guaranteed to them. The states of the Simla Hills were acquired after the war with Nepal, and the Mahratta Jaghirdars were the officers and subordinates of the Peishwa. In Bundelkand only three states have direct treaty rights; the others hold their territory under Ikrarnamahs or deeds of Allegiance. The engagements with states held under the Ikrarnamahs are generally alike. They declare generally, 'that the territory was acquired by cession from the Peishwa (or any other sovereign ruler as the case may be) and *annexed* to British dominions, but that the states of the chiefs were continued to them out of motives of justice, benevolence and good faith. They bind the chiefs to implicit submission, loyalty and attachment to the British Government. . . . They are liable to such control as the British Government may see fit to exercise and the rights and powers of the chiefs are limited to those that have been expressly *conferred*.'[1] How far the rights of these chiefs who hold their territory under Ikrarnamah are limited can be seen from the following clauses of the Deed of Allegiance, dated 29th October, 1846, executed by Rajah Ram Singh of Nalagad :

> I recognise the right of the people to appeal to the local British agent against oppression and injustice. I engage on pain of forfeiture of the grant to pay implicit obedience to any advice or remonstrance which the British agent may have occasion to offer on their behalf.[2]

In another grant it is declared :

> Be it known that the grant has been made on condition of good behaviour and of service military and political at any time of general danger or disturbance.

It is clear that the source, extent and nature of the rights possessed by these states differ fundamentally from the rights of ruling states. These rulers who hold under Ikrarnamah have *no* sovereignty of any kind, and their authority is derivative and not inherent. Their rule was continued ' by grace,' and they hold their territory subject to conditions made explicit in the Ikrarnamah. They have military and political obligations, and the residuary rights do not belong to them. Their subjects have the right of direct appeal. The political tie is feudal, and is not based on reciprocal obligations.

[1] Aitchison, vol. v. p. 17.

[2] *Ibid.* vol. viii. p. 325.

APPENDIX II

NOTE I

Treaty with the Nizam

Treaty of perpetual and general defensive alliance, between the Honourable the English East India Company and His Highness the Nabob Nizam ul Mulk Asoph Jah Bahadur Soubahdar of the Deccan, his children, heirs and successors; settled by Captain James Achilles Kirkpatrick, Resident at the Court of His Highness by virtue of the powers delegated to him by the most noble Richard Marquess Wellesley, etc., etc.

Whereas, by the blessing of God, an intimate friendship and union have firmly subsisted for a length of time between the Honourable Company and His Highness the Nabob Nizam ul Mulk Asoph Jah Bahadur and have been cemented and strengthened by several treaties of alliance to the mutual and manifest advantage of both powers, who with uninterrupted harmony and concord, having equally shared the fatigues and dangers of war and the blessings of peace are in fact become one and the same in interest, policy, friendship and honour. These powers, adverting to the complexion of the times have determined, on principles of precaution and foresight, and with a view to the effectual preservation of constant peace and tranquillity to enter into a defensive alliance, for the complete and reciprocal protection of their respective territories, together with those of their several allies and dependents, against the unprovoked aggressions or unjust encroachments of all or any enemies whatever.

Article 1. The peace union and friendship, so long subsisting between the states, shall be perpetual ; the friends and enemies of either shall be friends and enemies of both ; and the contracting parties agree that all former treaties and agreements between the two states, now in force and not contrary to the tenor of this agreement, shall be confirmed by it.

Article 2. If any power or state whatever shall commit any act of unprovoked hostility or aggression against either of the contracting parties or against their respective dependents or allies, and after due representation shall refuse to enter into amicable explanation, or shall deny the just satisfaction or indemnity which the contracting parties shall have required, then the contracting parties will proceed to concert and prosecute such further measures as the case shall appear to demand.

For the more distinct explanation of the intent and purpose of this agreement, the Governor-General in Council on behalf of the Company hereby declares that the British Government will never permit any power or state whatever to commit with impunity any act of unprovoked hostility or aggression against the rights or territories of His Highness the Nizam, but will at all times maintain the same, in the same manner as the rights and territories of the Honourable Company are now maintained.

Article 3. With a view to fulfil this treaty of general defence and protection, His Highness the Nabob Asoph Jah agrees that two battalions of sepoys and one regiment of cavalry with a due proportion of guns and artillerymen shall be added in perpetuity to the present permanent subsidiary force of six battalions of sepoys of one thousand firelocks each and one regiment of cavalry five hundred strong (with their proportion of guns and artillerymen) so that the whole subsidiary force furnished by the Hon'ble the East India Company to His Highness shall henceforward consist of eight battalions of sepoys (or eight thousand firelocks) and two regiments of cavalry (or one thousand horse) with their requisite complement of guns, European artillerymen, Lascars and pioneers fully equipped with warlike stores and ammunition; which force is to be stationed in perpetuity in His Highness's territories.

Article 4. The pay of the above-mentioned additional force shall be calculated at the rate of pay of the existing subsidiary force and shall commence from the day of the entrance of the said additional force into His Highness's territories.

Article 5. (Territory assigned for payment.)

Article 6. (Territory exchanged.)

Articles 7 *to* 12. (Details of territorial exchange.)

Article 12. The contracting parties will employ all practical means of conciliation to prevent the calamity of war; and for that purpose, will at all times be ready to enter into amicable explanations with other states, and to cultivate and improve the general relations of peace and amity with all the powers of India, according to the true spirit and tenor of this defensive treaty; but if a war should unfortunately break out between the contracting parties and any other power whatever then His Highness the Nabob Asoph Jah engages that with the reserve of two battalions of sepoys, which are to remain near His Highness's person the residue of the British subsidiary forces joined by six thousand infantry and nine thousand horse of His Highness's own troops and making together an army of twelve thousand infantry and ten thousand cavalry with their requisite train of artillery and warlike stores of every kind shall be immediately put into motion for the purpose of opposing the enemy, and His Highness further engages to bring into the field as speedily as possible, the whole force which he may be able to supply from his dominions with a view to the effectual prosecution and the speedy termination of the said war, the Honourable Company in the same manner engaging on their part in this case to employ in active operations against the enemy the largest force they may be able to furnish over and above the said force.

Article 13. (Deals with collection of stores.)

Article 14. (About grain and other provision to be supplied by the Nizam.)

Article 15. As by the present treaty the union and friendship of the two states are so firmly cemented as that they may be considered one and the same, His Highness the Nizam engages neither to commence nor to pursue in future any negotiations with any other power whatever without giving previous notice and entering into mutual consultation with the Hon'ble East India Company's government; and the Hon'ble Company's government on their part declare that they have no manner of concern with any of His Highness's children, relations, subjects or servants with respect to whom His Highness is absolute.

Article 16. As, by the present treaty of general defensive alliance, mutual defence and defence against all enemies are established His Highness the Nabob Asoph Jah consequently engages never to commit any act of hostility or aggression against any power whatever; and in the event of differences arising whatever adjustment of them, the Company's government, weighing matters in the scale of truth and justice, may determine shall meet with full approbation and acquiescence.

Article 17. (About collection of taxes by the Nizam from Sholapur and Gudwall Zamindars and the right to use the subsidiary force against them in cases of default.)

Article 18. Whereas by the favour of Providence a perfect understanding, harmony and concord have long and firmly subsisted between the Hon'ble East India Company His Highness the Nawab Asoph Jah, His Highness the Peishwa Rao Pandit Pradhan Bahadur, and Rajah Raghoji Bonsalah, therefore, should His Highness Rao Pandit Pradhan and Rajah Raghaji Bonsalah or either of them express a desire to participate in the benefits of the present defensive alliance which is calculated to strengthen and perpetuate the foundations of general tranquillity, the contracting parties will readily admit both or either of the said powers to be members of the present alliance on such terms and conditions as shall appear just and expedient to the contracting parties.

Article 19. The contracting parties being actuated by a sincere desire to promote and maintain general tranquillity, will admit Dowlut Rao Scindia to be a party to the present treaty whenever he shall satisfy the contracting parties of his disposition to cultivate the relations of peace and amity with both states and shall give such securities for the maintenance of tranquillity as shall appear to the contracting parties to be sufficient.

Article 20. (Deals with the ratification and exchange of the document.)

Signed, Sealed and Exchanged at Hyderabad on the 12th October A.D. 1800, on 22nd Jammadie ul Awul Anno Higerea 1215.

Signed : J. A. Kirkpatrick.

NOTE II.

The Udaipur Treaty

Treaty between the Honourable the English East India Company and Maharana Bheemsingh Rana of Udaipur, concluded by Mr. Theophilus Metcalfe on the part of the Hon'ble Company in virtue of full powers granted by His Excellency the most Noble the Marquis of Hastings, K.G., Governor-General and Thakoor Ajeet Singh on the part of the Maharana in virtue of full powers conferred by the Maharana aforesaid.

Article 1.

There shall be perpetual friendship alliance and unity of interests between the two states from generation to generation and the friends and enemies of one shall be friends and enemies of both.

Article 2.

The British Government engages to protect the principality and territory of Oudeypore.

Article 3.

The Maharana of Oudeypore will always act in subordinate co-operation with the British Government and acknowledge its supremacy and will not have any connection with other chiefs or states.

Article 4.

The Maharana of Oudeypore will not enter into any negotiation with any chief or state without the knowledge and sanction of the British Government; but his usual amicable correspondence with friends and relations shall continue.

Article 5.

The Maharana of Oudeypore will not commit aggressions upon any one; and if by accident a dispute arise with any one it shall be submitted to the arbitration and award of the British Government.

Article 6.

One-fourth of the revenues of the actual territory of Oudeypore shall be paid annually to the British Government as tribute for five years; and after that term three-eighths in perpetuity. The Maharana will not have any connection with any other power on account of tribute; and if any one advance claims of that nature the British Government engages to reply to them.

Article 7.

Whereas the Maharana represents that portions of the dominions of Oudeypore have fallen by improper means into the possession of others and solicits the restitution of those places ; the British Government from want of accurate information is not able to enter into any positive engagement on this subject, but will always keep in view the renovation of the prosperity of the state of Oudeypore and after ascertaining the nature of each case will use its best exertions for the accomplishment of that object on every occasion on which it may be proper to do so. Whatever places may thus be restored to the state of Oudeypore, by the aid of the British Government three-eighths of their revenue shall be paid in perpetuity to the British Government.

Article 8.

The troops of the state of Oudeypore shall be furnished according to its means, at the requisition of the British Government.

Article 9.

The Maharana of Oudeypore shall always be absolute ruler in his own country and the British jurisdiction shall not be introduced into that principality.

Article 10.

The present treaty of ten articles, having been concluded at Delhi and signed and sealed by Mr. Charles Theophilus Metcalfe and Thakoor Ajeet Singh Bahadur the ratifications of the same by His Excellency the Most Noble the Governor-General and Maharana Bheemsingh shall be mutually delivered within a month from this date.

Signed : C. T. Metcalfe.
Signed : Thakoor Ajeet Singh.
Signed : Hastings.

Ratified by His Excellency the Governor-General this 22nd day of January, 1818 in camp Oocher.

Signed : J. Adam,
Secretary to Governor-General.

NOTE III

(The following is a sample of the Fael Zamin executed by the Kathiawad chiefs.)

Fael Zamin of the Chief of Gondal.

Written by Barot Karar son of Fulsji Rupsinghji of Nara to Shrimant Rao Sir Sena Khas Khel Shamsher Bahadoor.

To wit,—That I, of my own free will have given to the Shrimant Pandit Pradhan and to the government of the Gaekwar on behalf of Jadeja Dwaji and Kunwar Natuji of the Taluka Gondal Dhoraji constant and efficient security against exciting disturbances (fael zamin) for the two shares constituting the entire province as follows :

Article 1.

That I will not have a feud with any other (Thalukdar) nor will I harbour the outlaws of any other (Thalukdar) whether Kathi or Rajput nor will incite any other person to commit any act of violence, nor will I encroach upon the boundary of another. I agree to act as has been the custom hitherto if any one's Bhayat should come and write over to me their lands or village, I will not purchase such lands or village. I will not revenge myself upon any one of my past enemities. I will not harbour thieves in my limits, but if I keep any in my country it shall be under proper precautions. I will not plunder in the Thaluka of any other chief or on the high road. If any impoverished landholder should be in want, and write over his land or village, I shall report the matter to government and only purchase them after obtaining permission. And if I should ever wish to write over my lands to any one I will only write them over after obtaining the government permission.

Article 2.

I will not associate with any delinquent or criminal of government whether one of the Shreemant Shree's government or of the Company Bahadur's.

Article 3.

On both sides of us are situated the Mahats of the Shrimant Pant Pradhan and the Gaekwar government and also those of the Honourable Company. In these Mahats I will not commit any robberies or make any plundering incursions nor will I in any way molest any merchant or traveller but will supply them with labourers and guards and thus escort them beyond my frontier. The owner of the village, within the limits of which a merchant or traveller may suffer loss shall be responsible for the same and if the loss be sustained in the village of a Thalukdar the Thalukdar shall be responsible and shall produce the real thief.

Article 4.

If I have encroached on the frontier of any other (Zamindar) by force or purchased the land of any one knowing him to be impoverished, then I agree to assign such land on fair terms and afterwards make no claim for it.

Article 5.

According to the above conditions I execute this deed and make Jamsu Jasaji of the Navanagar Taluka counter security for it ; and agree to fulfil the (terms of the) same as above. Should the Sarkar's mohsal come on account of any failure to observe this agreement, then I consent to give such satisfaction of the case in point as the Sarkar and their officials may demand and together with the daily expenses and fine imposed by the mohsal—Kartak Sudh 22nd Samvat, 1864.

Signature of the Security.

Signature of the Counter Security.

A SHORT BIBLIOGRAPHY

A COMPREHENSIVE bibliography in the case of a subject like this is impossible. A vast amount of material lies buried in the departmental records of the Government of India, and the various Indian states. Many of the important despatches and memoranda are published, but a great deal is still considered confidential. So far as the formal treaties, agreements and sanads are concerned the foreign department of the Government of India has issued an authorised publication which is an invaluable mine of information on all topics connected with the Indian states. The work is entitled :

A Collection of Treaties, Engagements and Sanads relating to India and Neighbouring Countries. By SIR CHARLES AITCHISON. Revised by the Authority of the Foreign Department of the Government of India (4th Edition, 1909, Calcutta).

Of other published books the following I have found very valuable :

1. *A Historical Sketch of the Princes of India.* JOHN CLUNES. Edinburgh, MDCCCXXXIII.
2. *The Imperial Gazetteer.* Vol. IV.
3. *Wellesley Papers.* OWEN. Clarendon Press.
4. *Select Writings of Elphinstone.* FORREST.
5. *Bombay Gazetteer.* CAMPBELL.
6. *The House of Scindia.* JOHN HOPE. Longmans & Green, 1863.

7. *The Guicwar and His Relations with the British Government.* Col. R. Wallace. Bombay, 1863.

8. *Central India.* By Sir J. Malcolm.

9. *A History of Travancore.* By Sankunny Menon. Madras, 1887.

10. *Nagam Aiyya.* Travancore State Manual, Trevandum.

11. *Currencies of the Hindu States of Rajputana.* By William Wilfrid Webb. London, 1893.

12. *Forces of the Native States of India.* Anonymous. London, 1879.

13. *A Plea for the Princes of India.* By J. Sullivan. London, 1853.

14. *A Letter to the Right Hon'ble Sir John Hobhouse on the Impolicy of Destroying the Native States of India.* J. Sullivan. London, 1850.

15. *Are we Bound by our Treaties?* J. Sullivan. London, 1852.

16. *Adoption* versus *Annexation.* V. N. Mandalik. London, 1866.

17. *Facts connected with the Dethronement of the Nawab of Tonk.* J. T. Pritchard.

18. *The Story of Satara.* By Major Basu. Panini Press, Allahabad.

19. *Oriental Annual.* 1809.

20. *Biographies*, in the 'Rulers of India' Series (Clarendon Press) of:

(i) Dalhousie,
(ii) Canning,
(iii) Mayo.

21. *Lord Curzon's Speeches in India.*

22. *Lord Chelmsford's Speeches in India.*

23. *Sir Henry Maine.* A brief memoir by the Rt. Honourable Sir M. E. Grant-Duff. John Murray, 1892.

24. *The Life of Dewan Sankara Warrier.* By C. ATCHUTA MENON TRICHUR. 1923.

25. *The Life of Dewan Sankunni Menon.* By C. ATCHUTA MENON TRICHUR. 1924.

26. *Our Indian Protectorate.* CHARLES LEWIS TUPPER. London, 1893.

27. *British Treatment of Indian Princes.* 'Westminster Review,' January, 1863.

28. *Modern India.* SIR GEORGE CAMPBELL. London, 1852.

29. *The Protected Princes of India.* SIR WILLIAM LEE WARNER.

30. *The Army in India and its Evolution.* Supt. Government Printing Press, Calcutta, 1924.

31. *History of Kerala.* K. P. PADMANABHA MENON. Cochin Government Press, 1924.

32. *The Rajas of the Punjab.* LEPPIL GRIFFIN.

33. *International Law in Ancient India.* S. V. VISWANATH. Longmans, 1925.

34. *Historical Sketch of Southern Mahratta Country.* MAJOR E. W. WEST. Bombay, 1878.

35. *Nizam, His History and Relations with the British Government.* 2 vols. H. G. BRIGGS. London, 1861.

36. *Nizam, Our Faithful Ally.* CAPTAIN FRAZER. London, 1865.

37. *Brief History of the Bhopal Principality.* HOUGH. Calcutta, 1845.

38. *Chapters of Oudh History.* H. C. IRWIN. London, 1880.

39. *Papers relative to the Progress of British Power in India and the Subsidiary System of Alliance.* B. S. JONES. London, 1832.

40. *Central India during the Mutiny.* DR. LOWE. London, 1860.

41. *The History of Bhawalpur.* SHAHMET ALI. London, 1848.

INDEX